Fit In!

Also by Mark A. Williams

The 10 Lenses: Your Guide to Living & Working in a Multicultural World
(Capital, 2001)

Your Identity Zones: Who Am I? Who Are You? How Do We Get Along?
(Capital, 2004)

Other Titles in the Capital Ideas for Business & Personal Development Series:

BE HEARD THE FIRST TIME: The Woman's Guide to Powerful Speaking
by Susan Miller

MANAGER MECHANICS: People Skills for First-time Managers
by Eric P. Bloom

MENTAL AGILITY: The Path to Persuasion by Robert L. Jolles

*MILLION DOLLAR NETWORKING: The Sure Way to Find, Grow and
Keep Your Business* by Andrea Nierenberg

THE NEW TALK POWER: The Mind-Body Way to Speak like a Pro
by Natalie H. Rogers

NONSTOP NETWORKING: How to Improve Your Life, Luck, and Career
by Andrea Nierenberg

NOW WHAT DO I DO? The Woman's Guide to a New Career
by Jan Cannon

THE POWER OF HANDSHAKING: For Peak Performance Worldwide
by Robert E. Brown and Dorothea Johnson

*THE SAVVY PART-TIME PROFESSIONAL: How to Land, Create,
or Negotiate the Part-Time Job of Your Dreams* by Lynn Berger

SOLD! Direct Marketing for Real Estate Professionals by Lois K. Geller

Save 25% when you order any of these and other fine Capital titles from
our Web site: www.capital-books.com.

  Fit In!

Fit In!

THE UNOFFICIAL GUIDE TO CORPORATE CULTURE

MARK A. WILLIAMS

Capital Ideas for
Business & Personal
Development

CAPITAL
BOOKS, INC.

Capital Books, Inc.
Sterling, Virginia

Capital Books, Inc.

P.O. Box 605

Herndon, Virginia 20172-0605

ISBN 10: 1-933102-37-3   (alk. paper)

ISBN 13: 978-1-933102-37-5

Library of Congress Cataloging-in-Publication Data

Library of Congress Cataloging-in-Publication Data

Williams, Mark Alexander

   Fit in! : the unofficial guide to corporate culture / Mark A. Williams.

      p. cm.Includes index.

   ISBN-13: 978-1-933102-37-5 (alk. paper)

   ISBN-10: 1-933102-37-3 (alk. paper)

   1. Corporate culture. 2. Organizational behavior. 3. Communication in organizations. 4. Success in business. I. Title.

   HD58.7.W545 2007

   650.1--dc22

                                2006033149

Printed in the United States of America on acid-free paper that meets the American National Standards Institute Z39-48 Standard.

First Edition

10 9 8 7 6 5 4 3 2 1

In memory of my mentors
Gloria Fauth and Raymond Whitfield
who always made me feel at home
in their presence

Acknowledgments

I'd like to acknowledge Mel Warriner, a colleague and friend who has always embraced my work and answered calls for support. This time he helped me find the poetry in introducing the "P"analogies in this book. His keen insight and masterful ability to frame complex issues so that they are easy to understand and capture deeper meaning are vital gifts he has been uniquely blessed with.

I'd also like to thank Laurie Williams, my wife, who also sacrificed early mornings and hours of sleep providing positive feedback, reading drafts, contributing ideas, and editing. Her unconditional support and encouragement are the fuels that keep me going.

The idea to translate *Fit In!* into parable style is credited to my friend and colleague Donna Oetzel whose insight and instinct were invaluable to this project. Special thanks also go to Joe Gibbons at the Future Work Institute for his support in framing the research questions.

And finally, there would be no "Simply Secrets" parable without Evan Harvey. His dedication, creativity, criticism, writing, polishing, coaching, and editing contributions to this project are immense. I enjoyed working with Evan and look forward to working with him on future projects.

Many thanks to my agents Muriel Nellis and especially Jane Roberts who saw the little gem that was present within my original drafts. I am blessed to have benefited from their wisdom and love.

Contents

Foreword

I've been asked to share a few words about *Fit in! The Unofficial Guide to Corporate Culture*. Here they are: Enlightening, Tangible, Action-oriented, Funny, Fun, Entertaining, and Totally Correct!! In this book Mark Williams has taken the notion of corporate culture and reduced it to bite-sized pieces to facilitate digestion at all levels of corporate America. Consider these few thoughts regarding the "few words" about the book.

Totally Correct: Mark knows that I work in a high level executive search firm; and in that context, we are constantly finding leading executives for mid-cap companies right up through the Fortune 10. Consider that assessing candidates' varied capabilities to actually execute the role we seek to fill is critical, but is only half of the effort. The other half of the work we do (at great time and expense) is assessing the candidates' abilities to fit in with our client's culture, and their abilities to drive the identified business initiatives successfully through that culture.

Enlightening: On a different note, we search consultants are constantly called to advise leading executives about their careers and career choices.

"Should I wait here for the promotion, or leave and start afresh?"

"Is this the right fit for me?"

"Am I earning what I should be?"

"I've been passed over again, how should I read that?"

Mark's framework can help answer these questions specifically and quantitatively.

Tangible: The insights and answers to both assessing likely/potential fit, as well as assessing current career standing are contained in *Fit In!* Mark has managed to create an easy-to-manage framework for considering and assessing one's culture fit. The framework is structured to facilitate a quick review, to be easy to understand, and to get straight to the point.

Action-oriented: Mark provides specific examples of the Fit Factors offered within the framework. He even includes the fact-finding questions to ask/observe about the company to assess one's culture fit. The Fit Assessment at the end of the book gives the reader a step-by-step methodology for effectively employing the framework. And, if that is not enough, Mark has integrated all of this in an interactive experience on his Web site. He leaves very little room for lack of action.

Funny, Fun, and Entertaining: I love fun! Mark made this book fun to read. While I was reading it, I laughed out loud through the first chapter. The way Mark describes Simply Secrets, Inc. was hysterical—the company has everything, but can disclose nothing since its business is secrets—conference rooms no one has ever seen, high-powered executives who cannot be named . . . what a hoot! Even the footnotes consistently add to the fun.

At the end of the day, Mark has placed in each reader's hands the ability to:

- Consider the culture fit within the current employer/company (to support a stay/leave decision);

- Consider, and even quantitatively assess, the likely fit within a potential employer/company;

- Sharpen the vision/insight into which *specific* dynamics affect/drive all of the above.

This book and the framework herein can be used to guide one's own path even in a steady-state mode. The insights included can better focus one's attention on the right dynamics to observe and subsequently manage. Mid-level managers can use this framework to shape the perceptions and reputations that follow them and redirect those perceptions to lead to the career movement they seek.

The Fit Assessment can even support executives who are interviewing new hires for the organizations they lead. Remember that once one becomes an integral part of an organization and its culture, it is so ingrained that it may not be as clear or distinct to those living within it. Thus, *Fit In!* can help such executives re-clarify exactly what their respective corporate cultures are and thereby facilitate their respective abilities to better assess the candidates they are interviewing.

Read *Fit In! The Unofficial Guide to Corporate Culture* and maximize the one aspect (albeit pervasive) of your career management plan that could have the most significant impact on successfully executing your plan.

—Sharon S. Hall, Partner
Spencer Stuart

How to Use This Book

I'd like you to do more than just read *Fit In!* Use it as a guidebook, a toolkit, and a starting point for more knowledge. If you're looking for a job, reevaluating your current position, or still in search of that elusive dream, this book offers practical advice. But it also empowers HR executives, leaders, and managers to do their jobs better. *Fit In!* can help you assess employee dynamics and strategize ways to get them back on track.

Fit In! is organized into four main sections. In the first, I talk about my personal history, lay out the origins of this book, and introduce some of the main concepts. I want you to understand why fit matters before we see it in action. In the second section, I'll relate a brief and (hopefully) entertaining parable. I found that this was the best way to bring complexity into the discussion without getting bogged down in rhetoric and explanation—different characters tend to express different viewpoints better than any single individual could. Third, we'll analyze the parable as it unfolds, exposing the dynamics behind character interactions. As you spot the forces at work in this story, then you will certainly become better able to spot similar trends in your own environment. Finally, I have included appendix material that focuses on key aspects of the fit experience: human resources management, cultural scanning, and strategies for dealing with fit conflict.

There's another reason why I use a parable in this book: because I want you to be part of the story. Imagine yourself in the room, hearing what the others hear, trying your best to understand and express your own opinions. Organizations often rise and fall based on backroom deals and informal discussions. I want you to have a front row seat as this plays out.

Ultimately, we all must live and work in the real world—where answers are hard-won and complexities ever-present. I am a big believer in research; it helps us understand real world situations and attitudes. I commissioned a great deal of research for this project; you will see some of it in this book. It should ground these ideas in reality, and drive you to do even more work on your own, after you close these covers.

So I encourage you to do your own research, read other books, come to our Web site, take the diagnostic tests, discuss these ideas with friends and family—in short, learn everything you can. Knowledge gained is twice as powerful as knowledge given. I wrote *Fit In!* to open the door, but you have to walk inside.

Fit In!

Chapter 1

The Unspoken Rules

M ost likely, there will come a point in your career when your ability to "prove" your competence to meet the requirements of a new job will not be in question; rather, you will have to compete to prove that you fit *into* the culture of the business. Contemplate this scenario: You go up for a great job against two other candidates. The three of you are equally qualified, competent, and experienced. Who lands the job? How is that decision made? The answers to these questions are at the heart of "Fit In."

Based on over twenty-five years of executive and organizational consulting, I've learned these decisions come down to a matter of what I call *fit*. By fit I mean the elusive match between your profile and that specific combination of unspoken and informal social, behavioral, and cultural criteria unique to every organization. By answering questions such as "who do I feel comfortable with?" and "who seems most natural in the role?" or "who's most likely to blend into our culture?" your next employer will determine who gets the job. In fact, once beyond entry-level positions, your advancement and success depend heavily on your ability to understand and master these unwritten rules. Few of us can readily decode or quickly master them, however, before opportunity slips away. So, it becomes very important to learn all about these hidden rules I call "Fit Factors."

Cracking the Code

Not everything that happens in a business is based on visible, objective, and formal rules. Some things are more subtle; they live between the lines of the company manual. These informal rules are a powerful hidden force—governing everything from where you sit in a meeting to how you address your superiors. It's difficult to grasp the nuances of informal rules because they are only silently acknowledged.

When do people typically discover these unspoken rules? You can be warned, counseled or given advice by an ally trying to help you from the inside, or you can observe others in action and begin to mimic them, or worse, you can unknowingly violate the rules and suffer the consequences. Or you can adjust your lenses and learn to scan cultures in a different way. Read how I once learned to "fit in" with a former client of mine!

I'm Only Trying to Help

I was preparing to meet with the CEO of a Fortune 100 company that was one of my best clients. At that time, I carried an appointment calendar featuring pictures of Hawaii and I loved it because it reminded me of my favorite retreat spot.

I was warned by a senior executive at the company that I could not go to the CEO meeting with this calendar because it would look "unprofessional." I was unmoved by his advice because in my mind, the kind of calendar I used had nothing to do with the quality of my advice. Everyone in this particular company used Day-Timers"! No one at this company specifically required you to carry a Day-Timer, nor was it a formal, written policy in the Employee Handbook. But the Day-Timers carried by all the executives were thick and tidy, and had their names embossed on the cover with a gold plaque. The Day-Timer was an "informal rule" developed to reinforce the company's value on organization, neatness, and structure—all distinguishing qualities of this corporation's culture.

About a week before my scheduled meeting with the CEO, a box addressed to me arrived containing a brand new Day-Timer. Enclosed was this note: "I'm only trying to help." Well, certainly if it was this important for my client to purchase and send me the Day-Timer at his own expense, I thought I had better use it. And so I did. At the meeting with the CEO, I took the Day-Timer as a prop. I kept it afterward for many months as a kind of non-verbal reminder of the importance of informal rules.

Other examples of informal norms can include:

- *Vacation time:* How many consecutive days can you take off before losing credibility?
- *Contributions:* When they knock on your door to donate to company causes and outside political groups, how should you respond?
- *Communications:* Who and when do you copy others on e-mail and phone communications?
- *Dress:* How expensive and stylish should your work wardrobe be?
- *Time:* What time are you "really" expected to arrive and leave work?

- *Credit:* When do you take the credit for success versus giving it to your boss or team?
- *Neighborhoods:* How close to others at your level are you expected to live?
- *Decorations:* What kind of pictures of family and friends, and personal items should you have on your desk or in your office?
- *Access to superiors:* Is there really an open door policy? Can you circumvent the chain of command?
- *At-home access:* Is your off-time really your own or are you expected to be available 24/7?
- *Exposure:* Is it wise to be on special projects and get visibility?
- *Directness:* Are you expected to voice disagreements in real time or behind closed doors?
- *Saying no:* Are you really ""free"" to turn down that offer or would that be a career ender?
- *Your significant other:* Do they have to fit in and be accepted because of public aspects of your job?
- *The Loop:* Do you have to have a meeting before the real meeting to let others know where you stand?
- *Team player:* At what point must you get on board and salute?

These are just some examples of the intangible, hidden norms buried in the fabric of your business, used to help the decision makers sort out affinity; in other words, do you walk, talk, and behave like one of us! These informal rules are established over time with many points of input. Sometimes the personalities and preferences of the founder and significant players set the tone. Industry norms and standards can also play a part, as well as professional and cultural preferences for how to get things done. Wherever they come from, adherence to these informal rules can determine your success (or failure) in a business.

In *Fit In* you'll find everything you need to identify your company's informal "Fit Factors" and determine what is expected of you to be successful. You'll also take a look at those aspects of yourself you'd be willing to compromise to fit in.

Or perhaps, you'll determine you don't want to compromise and decide it's best to find another opportunity where your unique style and contributions will be recognized and valued.

Job Posting! New President of the United States

Do you meet the formal written criteria to be the President of the United States of America? Section One of Article Two of the United States Constitution establishes the legal requirements of the Office of the President. The president must be a natural-born citizen of the United States (or a citizen at the time the Constitution was adopted), be at least thirty-five years old, and have been a resident of the United States for fourteen years. That's it. That's the *stated criteria*, i.e. the formal rules. The reality is that we have collectively and silently developed a set of "informal rules" about who should be president that have been institutionalized unofficially over time. See if you recognize these rules and remember, there are always exceptions, but overall these are the informal criteria:

Informal Criteria to become President of the United States of America:

- Military experience
- Legal experience
- Member of a political party
- Charismatic
- Strong
- Wealthy
- Highly educated
- Male
- White
- Experience as former elected official
- Decisive
- Family man
- Christian

As you review these criteria, think about how these informal rules are advantageous for members of some identity groups and disadvantageous for others. An "identity group" is a grouping of people who share certain similarities such as race, gender, religion, age, level of education, and social class.

Now, ask yourself how many of the informal, unwritten criteria you meet? How many people do you personally know who meet all of them? Many of the informal criteria are *style and group membership* elements we have come to accept as "conventional wisdom." Many informal norms also represent bias—excluding someone with a different style, different work experiences, or a different approach that could also do the job. For example in the 1960s, for the first time Americans elected a president who was Catholic; and in the early 1990s, we elected a modern era president who had not served in the military.

If you look at the list of informal norms related to serving as President of the United States in relation to the stated criteria written formally in the Constitution, it demonstrates just how powerful informal norms are and why it is important to learn to decode them.

Fitting the Physical Image

- In 1960, John Kennedy inserted the requirement that both candidates stand in the televised debate to exploit the fact that Richard Nixon had sprained his knee. Nixon shifted his weight during the debates, an action that looked uncertain and nervous.
- Jimmy Carter demanded a smaller lectern to stand behind in order to mask his shorter height. In return, President Ford was permitted to pick a background color that would mask the fact that he was balding.
- Michael Dukakis, six inches shorter than Vice President George H.W. Bush, arranged in 1988 to stand on a ramp that would raise him up to Bush's height.
- George H.W. Bush preferred to stand on the right side of the stage to hide his receding hair line.
- Televised debates favor politicians who are able to appear charming and at ease while on the stage. Kennedy trounced a sweating Nixon in 1960.
- Clinton played to the audience in 1992 by stepping off the debate stage and into the crowd.

Such tactics underlie an understanding of the way people evaluate and judge if a candidate meets certain criteria. While many people meet the formal stated criteria for filling the Office of the President, very few meet the informal criteria. That's what "fit" is all about.

The Gold Standard

When I was in my early twenties, I was part of a consulting team that pitched a client for a big account. At the time, the client was one the biggest financial institutions in New York. Our consulting team was really on fire that day; I was certain we would win the account.

One week later, however, word came that we had not won. Disappointed and confused, I asked one of my colleagues why she thought it hadn't gone our way.

Though reluctant, she eventually explained. I was shocked to discover that the problem lay in a small, seemingly trivial detail of my physical appearance. Believe it or not, it all came down to a single tooth.

I had chipped one of my front teeth when I was twelve years old, "skating" in my socks on the hardwood floors of my house. Thanks to a few reckless slides and a rogue splinter, I tumbled face-first onto the floor. The dentist fitted me with a temporary tooth cap that was white with a hairline gold rim. Rather than trading this cap later in life for something more up-to-date (minus the gold), I avoided dentists because of a dental phobia. This decision proved costly later because it was that gold rim that had lost us the consulting job. As my colleague confessed, the bank's vice president confided that senior leadership "just wouldn't feel comfortable" with me.

That was my first experience with one of the Fit Factors I call your *Physical Package*. In this example, business people didn't accept me as an executive consultant because they felt my dental work made me look outdated, unprofessional, and out of step with my peers. There was no question about my skill, competence, or passion as we had earned high marks for our presentation, approach, and experience—but so did our competitors. The bank team concluded they better fit the *Physical Package* of an executive consultant and in so, doing awarded them the contract. The bank had used the unspecified criteria of comfort and fit as a determining factor to tilt the decision away from us toward the other consultants.

Another one of the Fit Factors, *Personal Presence*, recently helped me land a contract with a large Midwestern company. This company was struggling with tough competitive forces and needed an infusion of energy and inspiration for their executive team. Although there were competent, experienced local firms available, we won the company over because of another Fit Factor, my *Personal Presence*. They wanted more than subject matter competence: they wanted *inspiration*.

Fit Happens

Fit Factor decisions are made every day in corporate America. They may or may not be legal or fair—but they are made. They are made both consciously and unconsciously because informal norms, systems, traditions, rewards, and punishments are embedded in the inner workings of the organizational culture. *Fit In!* prepares you to decode these dynamics and make clear choices based on all the informal fit criteria.

There are ten Fit Factors that operate in today's business culture. These will be described through a parable that is infused with real-life examples of how each operates. By recognizing and managing these factors, you will be better prepared to find the best fit for your true self. But be warned that while observation and experience have proven most of us have some negotiable "fit gap," there inevitably comes a point when too many factors can prevent a proper fit and that's when you start "swimming upstream." Then the issue becomes how big is the gap, and how willing or able are you to adjust and master the informal requirements. The answers to these questions are critical to understanding and managing a well-suited fit for positions in business life today.

The ten Fit Factors are:

- **Packaging** (your look, appearance, physical, and cultural attributes)
- **Pedigree** (your background, heritage, credentials)
- **Patronage** (your advocates, allies, friends in high places)
- **Perspective** (your point of view, values, beliefs)
- **Pastimes** (your leisure activities, social activities)
- **Passion** (your drive, ambition, will to succeed)
- **Presence** (your style, demeanor, attitude, charisma)
- **Potential** (your perceived raw talent, intelligence)
- **PR** (your image, reputation, aura)
- **Passages** (your pathways, tickets to be punched, ways up the corporate ladder)

The Many Levels of Fit

Fit challenges can occur at various levels and stages of your career. For college students and those new to the world of the work, your point of entry for potential "Fit Fights" will begin the moment you select an industry. As you become more seasoned and experienced, your fit challenges are typically more focused on a specific organization, department, or location.

Industry Fit

Industries have a way of attracting people who share preferences for certain informal norms. Your skill may apply to many kinds of industries, but your preferences for work style may be out of sync with the modus operandi of a particular industry.

Professional Fit

Same is true with professions—your aptitudes and abilities may have better suitability than your current profession. You'll always be surrounded by people you don't jell with if you don't fundamentally fit the norms of your chosen profession.

Organizational Fit

Sometimes it's not your industry or profession that is troublesome—it's your organization. This can often be remedied through research and reconnaissance before you make a dramatic leap.

Department Fit

Sometimes you don't even have to leave your organization; your best fit could mean simply changing departments. You'd be surprised how many leaders set the tone for a department and impose quirky preferences not common to the entire organization.

Level Fit

Don't be fooled into thinking that just because you fit at your current level, you'll find smooth sailing at the next step up the ladder. The requirements become more stringent as you move up, and the pressure increases to fit in completely before you get a set of keys to the executive suite.

Location Fit

I wish I had a dollar for every time a manager or executive who has been successful in one position in a particular city relocates dutifully—only to find the people, culture, and style at the new location of the same company as different as night and day, resulting in a "Fit Fight." Major issues arise when moving from coast to coast, from rural to urban, from overseas, and from corporate to the field.

The Prime Directive

"Resistance is futile."

—The Borg/*Star Trek: The Next Generation*

Strong organizational cultures are an important ingredient in the overall success of businesses. The goal of corporate culture is to assimilate all employees into a work style that is most conducive to efficiency and productivity in order to maximize profit or complete the organizational mission. To accomplish this, businesses must very quickly identify people who can easily fit into the organizational culture to keep the enterprise running smoothly. Too many quirky parts and the system will break down.

Examples of organizations that have successfully communicated their culture instilled from top to bottom are:

Starbucks: Commitment to a friendly environment creates customer joy in seeking the little daily pleasures of life.

The US Military: Commitment to order, discipline, consistency, and selflessness fosters identity with unit and team over the individual, leading to success and survival for all in dangerous situations.

Apple Computer: Commitment to solving the industry challenge of how to download free music with the approval of the music industry and its copyright concerns led to the creation of the iPod player and a win-win for consumers and industry.

The achievements of these corporations resulted partly because of strong corporate cultures known intrinsically to each employee. Successful cultures embed their informal rules, norms, and expectations into the organizational DNA. Certain corporate tendencies emerge because every system—recruiting, mentoring, training, advancement, compensation and rewards—all screen to identify those who will fit in with cultural expectations. The attributes of company founders, stars, and protégés become the accepted benchmarks. Those in the corporation are expected to fall in line and adopt these norms.

Swimming Upstream

Most companies are run by "big fish"—those who have mastered the game, paid their dues, and made it to the top. They are for the most part deeply, personally committed to the company; their very identity is tied to the organization and they'll take it very personally if you try to change it. When companies say they want "fresh blood"—new employees with original ways of thinking from outside perspectives—I am skeptical and suspicious; and I warn you that you should be too! It is very difficult to change organizational Fit Factors—like weeds, they cannot be killed unless you go to the root.

Successful companies don't mess around with the roots of their organization. In most cases, these new people with their fresh perspectives end up discredited, marginalized, or exiled. If I've heard it once, I've heard it a hundred times: "They brought me in to shake things up and now that I'm here, they want me to 'assimilate' and accept the way they've always done things." You bet they do! My experience has taught me that unless businesses are in severe crisis, leaders are extremely reluctant to entertain even a slight shift in culture. In fact, slight shifts seem like radical changes, shaking the very foundations of their corporate civilization.

When you're swimming upstream and feeling at odds with your corporate culture—i.e. you're in the middle of a "Fit Fight" —you have three choices.

1. You can muscle and buck your way through the system, holding onto your fresh perspective, hoping your powerful allies from above will protect you because of your unique abilities.

2. You can change aspects of your behavior in order to better fit.

3. You can find a different job where your authentic self will be better appreciated and honored.

You will lose time, energy, and self-esteem if you make the wrong choice. The Fit Factors are just the right tools to help you decide which choice serves you best.

When considering these three options, you may wonder why people stay in organizations where they don't fit. I've come to believe it's mostly because of fear: fear that they won't find another job, or they'll lose their house or car, or they won't be able to provide for their family. Some worry that they're not really that talented and, in fact, they conclude they're downright lucky to have any job at their age. Or people rationalize that they only have a few more years to go until . . . kids are gone, retirement. So, people stay put.

And then you may wonder, what becomes of their work life. They retire "on the job," so-to-speak, and become nay-sayers or constantly call in sick or silently sabotage ongoing team efforts. They embark on pointless crusades to change the company and to affect the corporate culture, often becoming physically and emotionally sick, becoming cynical and toxic, and losing their power in the process.

This sadly all-too-frequent scenario is a reflection of a bad "fit" resulting in a lose-lose game where no one is a winner. Addressing the issue of proper fit could help to salvage such a situation by recognizing the inherent problems on an individual and organizational basis.

Two Realties, Which Is Yours?

Paradise

You wake up to your alarm ringing and it feels like your head just hit the pillow. You begin to prepare for your day and think about all the exciting things in store for you at work. In your mind, you run through what you'd like to accomplish and wonder how you'll get through all of it, but you sure want to try.

You arrive at work and are greeted by colleagues you enjoy, respect, and trust. You go to meetings, make phone calls, answer e-mails, and everything just seems to click. Suddenly, you look at your watch and notice the work day is already over and you have spent an additional hour beyond what is expected in order to make more headway. A part of you wishes you could work a bit longer, but you realize you have to leave. On the way home, you think about how to steal a little more time at home to tie up some loose ends and get ready for tomorrow. Once you arrive home, you are energized by sharing the details of your work day with those near and dear to you, and you are intense and engaged in the retelling.

All is well; you are excited about the upward direction your career is headed. You also have a sense of the timetable and markers critical to your success, and you see yourself as "on point." You've earned the support you need to take on increasing critical business challenges; and you know if you hit a bump in the road, your mentors will be there to guide you. Your contribution is valued, you're a key player; and for the moment, you can't imagine working anyplace else. Here are a few other signs that you're "swimming with the tide." Are you or those you care about experiencing any of them now?

Swimming with the Tide

- *You get timely feedback* about a "problem" and support about how to deal with the challenges.
- *You get plum opportunities* for exposure to the "big fish" because your managers think about how to better position you.
- *You're in the loop*; you know what's about to happen before others do.
- *Your suggestions are valued*—and sought out.
- *You're a part of the give and take*—when issues are being debated, new ideas bounced around, trouble shooting, or strategizing.
- *You go above and beyond* and others depend on you in challenging situations to come through without being asked.

- *You have an idea of what's next* related to future opportunities and that you're being positioned.
- *Colleagues take care of you*—they monitor how hard you're working and offer to support you to lessen your load.
- *You are energized*, by the environment, your team, and the work you are doing.

Hell

You toss and turn all night every night, and wake up day-after-day feeling like you never slept. As you roll over, you realize your body aches; and you take just a few more moments in bed. As you think about your upcoming workday, you think about how to structure the endless hours to make it through. You will be able to take a coffee break at 10:00 that you can stretch into a half hour, and then retreat to your work space and return phone calls and e-mail for at least another hour. Maybe if you finish around 11:30, you'll be able to leave a little early for lunch, avoiding some of the colleagues you don't want to be stuck with. You've become quite good at avoiding certain projects that include people who push your buttons because they are not your supporters. You have also learned when to speak up because it is required, as well as to recognize the times it is best to keep your mouth shut because you could make matters worse.

You remember when you used to freely share your ideas and no one would pick up on them, only to have someone else get credit for claiming them weeks later. You recall when team members began going out to do things socially and not inviting you. Now when they ask you to come along with them, you suspect it's only out of guilt. Over the past several months, you realize that as you approach team members, conversations end just as you come closer. More and more you feel that maybe they are talking about you when you're not around.

You're also aware that months ago you stopped getting the juicy assignments. You replay the day you received the feedback that you were not a "team player" and that you weren't quite ready for that next promotion. You now just accept you will be the last on the list to have phone calls returned from people in other departments. And to make matters worse, you've suffered through a string of chronic illnesses, using up most of your sick leave. For a long time now, your friends have been advising you to look for a new job, get a fresh start. But do you really want to go through a job search again? Do you?

You may have experienced both sides of these two work scenarios in your own work history. You may even be experiencing them now. If you are in the midst of a Fit Fight, you know the battle can sap your energy and deflate your sense of self. The energy you would normally use to be productive is used to survive instead.

Here are a few other signs that you're swimming upstream. Are you or those you care about experiencing any of them now?

Swimming Upstream

- *You get feedback* about a "problem," but the real issue is very hard to pin down.

- *You don't get opportunities* for exposure to the big fish because your managers are afraid you'll embarrass them.

- *You're not usually included* in the informal gatherings the "special" people always know about; and when you are included, they discuss occasions when you were absent.

- *Your suggestions are ignored*—suggestions that, in your mind, are painfully correct; instead your team responds like you've lost your mind for even bringing up the idea.

- *They tiptoe around you*, sugar-coating their comments to your face, but you know they "work around you" and talk behind your back.

- *You begin to obsess* about whether you should stay or go, talking to friends, teachers, loved ones, gurus, and psychics.

- *You redo your resume* and activate the process to let them know you're considering a change.

- *You fool your team* at work, convincing them that you're just as engaged as ever. You stay within the lines.

- *You get a new job*, go in to resign, and everyone is shocked. They tell you how much they'll miss you and how you always spoke the truth, challenging them to see things differently.

Rigid Fit Requirements Lead to Exclusion of Talent!

If you are a manager or executive in a business, the "big picture" danger of enshrining *informal rules* and not revisiting them over time is that they may eliminate entire categories of people who were prematurely screened out to preserve the sacred norms. Many times people in "bad fit" situations are given performance feedback *guised as competencies*, when the reality is that they are in a Fit Fight. One of the best lines is "you have to improve your communications skills."

Over time, companies can demonstrate their capacity to loosen the grip and make exceptions to the norm. As already seen with the presidential exceptions, the same pattern can be true for businesses—exceptions to the informal rules can be made. But keep in mind that in the end, *they are only exceptions*, not the rule. Changing "narrow" informal criteria takes a burning platform, time, patience, and dogged determination. Unless you're a pioneer or trendsetter, this should not be your primary goal.

The Fit Parable,
Simply Secrets

Fit In! is organized in a way that is fun and practical. The journey begins with a parable about a fictitious company called Simply Secrets. Reading about the exploits of this company, you'll learn about all ten of the Fit Factors as they play out in the Simply Secrets culture. The story begins with a special meeting convened by the "Big Fish" to replace an executive who has abruptly quit the company. As you read the parable of Simply Secrets, follow along and assess how each of the ten Fit Factors is affecting you *right now*. In doing so, you'll learn the process of decoding the informal aspects of organizational culture. If you're a manager, think about employees on your team who may be struggling with the Fit Factors, swimming upstream or in a Fit Fight. You'll think of ways that you can more effectively reach out to them to help them understand how to swim in your organizational or team culture.

While Simply Secrets was created to make learning about the Fit Factors fun, the issues, agendas, and perspectives described during the executive session are deadly serious and real. If you have been in organizations for a while, you will recognize first hand just how true these perspectives can be. Some of the issues raised would never be stated "on the record," but intuitively you know such perspectives are voiced and such discussions take place every day.

The parable continues with a "Fit Gap Analysis" conducted on one of the characters you will meet in the parable. The Fit Gap Analysis is followed by practical steps you can immediately take to conduct your own analysis of your current work situation or as a guide to assess how the Fit Factors operate, and their potential impact on you.

Rate Your Current Fit

Before you read the Simply Secrets parable, rate each of the Fit Factors from 1-10 based on how each of them affects you right now in your current job. The Fit Factor statements relate to those informal, unwritten, and sometimes unspoken rules that you have to figure out and follow in order to fit in and advance in your workplace. Remember to rate each question from the perspective of your current job and the way it affects you. This is an abbreviated version of the official Fit Indicator, you'll find at www.identityonline.com.

How Do You Fit In?

Which of the following informal rules that operates within your organizational culture creates the greatest barriers to your advancement? Rank yourself from 1 (not very much) to 10 (quite a lot).

1. Passion

Your dedication to your job: your personal commitment, zest for the work you do, the ability to put work first with 24/7 availability, the willingness to relocate and go anywhere at any time, a desire and ability to volunteer, a low need for time off, and a desire to stay in touch and be productive while on vacation.

Rank ____

2. PR

Your ability to promote yourself: your ability to build your reputation across the office, to establish a positive persona (i.e., the "go-getter," the "wordsmith," the "tech genius"), and to be highly regarded by those who matter.

Rank ____

3. Presence

Your personal presence in the workplace: your style, manner of being, and your ability to master the "company style," including charisma, charm, wit, persuasiveness, sense of command, outgoingness, or public speaking ability.

Rank ____

4. Perspective

How the values, philosophy, and mindset of your organization align with your values: the ability to be a "total team player," echo the "executive" line, do things "the company way," be in step with the "politics" of senior leaders, and protect "sacred cows."

Rank ___

5. Potential

Your potential: your ability to be recognized as a "future star;" being seen as a "stand out" in school, residencies, or internships; being seen as a "rising star" by those inside and outside of your organization; and being viewed as having raw "talent" that can be molded to fit the company's norms.

Rank ___

6. Pathways

Your career path: having your tickets punched in the right jobs and in the proper sequence, paying your dues, having the right amount of tenure, coming from the right part of the organization, and following in the footsteps of former executives.

Rank ___

7. Patronage

Your ability to attract and maintain powerful senior support: your need for a mentor, protector, ally, or champion, or to be viewed as a "protégé" of someone important.

Rank ___

8. Package

Your visible physical presence: your physical attributes, such as attractiveness, size, race, ethnicity, gender, or physical ability/fitness.

Rank ____

9. Pedigree

Your background: the schools you attended, the family you came from, your social class or status, or the "recognized excellence" of the organization or other place you were before your current position.

Rank ____

10. Pastimes

Your activities outside of work: sports you play, if and where you worship, who you socialize with, your lifestyle, or the associations and networks you belong to.

Rank ____

Now as you follow the Simply Secrets parable, refer back to your own rankings and reflect on how the Fit Factors are playing out in your organization and how they affect you right now. After the parable, we'll begin the process of learning how to scan prospective employers so you'll learn how you can make sure your next job is a perfect match.

You're invited to visit the *Fit In!* web site at www.identity-online.com to take the full *Fit In!* diagnostic, and get a personal reading on your fit preferences and what they mean. You can also cast your vote to solve the Simply Secrets mystery! We'll tell you how at the end of the book. Have fun!

Chapter 2

Simply Secrets, Inc.

Simply Secrets is the largest modern business solely dedicated to keeping secrets. The company has offices all over the world, albeit in secret locations. I could tell you the most amazing things about the work we do, but most of it is classified information. Simply Secrets specializes in keeping secrets—so our customers don't have to.

Have you ever been put in the uncomfortable position of having to keep a confidence? Perhaps you were just dying to tell someone, but ethics and a sense of loyalty kept you quiet. It can be so frustrating to sit on the scoop and never spill the beans.

Well, that's where Simply Secrets comes in: You can safely tell us your secret, knowing that we guarantee, in writing, never to disclose it to a third party. You simply make an appointment, dish the dirt, and succumb to simple human nature. In fact, Simply

Secrets will accept and safely archive your own private secrets—whether they concern past indiscretions, risky behavior patterns, embarrassing comments, bad decisions, lapses in judgment, or family skeletons. (Note: Customers from very wealthy, deeply entrenched families may have to pay a slight upgrade fee for this service.)

For six of the past seven years, we have been outperforming all financial forecasts. Things have leveled off a bit during the last three quarters, but we are still the clear market leader in covert knowledge warehousing. Simply Secrets is highly regarded, highly profitable, and highly attractive to investors and financiers.

Our celebrity client list, were it actually disclosed, would knock your socks off. We regularly receive invitations from Oprah's people, the Fox News crew, and a very nice woman who works for Lou Dobbs. They all want to put a Simply Secrets spokesperson on television—presumably to disclose the very secrets that our clients have charged us with keeping. But we must graciously decline all offers, of course.

But with great success come great challenges. The company is now facing competition from foreign conglomerates, and there are significant organizational hurdles to overcome. We have had to rapidly expand our employee base in order to keep up, and it is difficult to achieve high standards and provide top quality at all levels. This has little to do with supply and demand—we are constantly flooded with applications from qualified candidates. So where do things go awry?

The nature of our business means that other businesses—those designed to steal, expose, or even publish people's secrets—are constantly on the prowl. There are mercenaries, rogue extortionists, vengeful politicians, and supermarket tabloids sifting through our trash and peeking through our windows. Simply Secrets could withstand them all—if it weren't for the leaks.

How We Work

Simply Secrets is organized into four broad divisions:

- Domestic Secrets focuses on personal, family, and celebrity secrets.
- Commercial Secrets concerns industrial and political secrets.
- Universal Secrets covers religious, mystical, and natural secrets.
- Top Secret Operations provides the organizational apparatus for the acquisition and timely release of secrets.

Note: Due to the sensitive nature of its work, we will not disclose anything else about the Operations Division. Suffice to say their handiwork can be seen in any number of newspapers, magazines, and press releases on any given day. They even cover blogs. Actually, we can neither confirm nor deny the penetration rate of the Operations Division into the blogosphere. But I am at liberty to relate a quick anecdote.

As you may know, our Vice President of Domestic Secrets (let's call him "Mr. X") recently resigned for undisclosed reasons. Mr. X released a statement that read, in part: "I make this decision of my own free will, with no malice toward anyone, and will be forever thankful for my experience at this company. But I am also eager to embrace a new opportunity elsewhere." Industry insiders saw through the charade. They knew that Mr. X was not leaving of his own accord; he had, in fact, been nudged out the door. So let's officially put the rumors to rest: Mr. X was not, nor would he ever be, Simply Secrets material.

But frankly, the resignation could not have come at a worse time. A rapid influx of new accounts has kept us busy, while our chief competitor—who shall remain nameless[1]—has stolen a few clients right out from under our noses. A few more junior executives have defected; morale has begun to dip. Simply Secrets now fosters two warring factions: those who want to stabilize the business and better serve our existing customers, and others who prefer to blaze newer, ever more secret trails in pursuit of profit and power.

---

[1] Deep Six, Ltd. Founded in 2004; Headquartered in Tallahassee, FL.

We turned to our Executive Board for support and guidance. If this group cannot effectively replace Mr. X and right the Simply Secrets ship, then no one could. They have gone to work right away, convening a secret session in the Chamber of Silence. Perhaps I should explain: The Chamber of Silence is a soundproof room surrounded by three-foot thick walls of glass and granite. It is impervious to all known surveillance technology. It is the most secret heart of our most secret facility, and that's where the Executive Board holds its secret sessions.

Of course, I have never actually seen the Chamber of Silence. No one has, outside of the ten men and women who comprise the Executive Board—and their identities are, of course, kept strictly confidential. Once daily, while the Executive Board is in secret session, a memo will be distributed that summarizes their activities. The memo is heavily censored, so one cannot be sure of the exact sequence of events, but an outline may be offered.

The Executive Board elects a subgroup of five members, called the Management Quintet, who are charged with assessing needs, assembling suitable candidates, facilitating interviews (conducted via telephonic hookup and two-way mirrors), and presenting an action plan to the entire Executive Board. Once the entire Executive Board signs off on the chosen one, the recommendation is sent to the Chairman of the Board in a sealed envelope that self-destructs within moments of being read.

The Chairman of the Board, whose identity is shrouded by rumor and subterfuge[2], acts by offering an official recommendation to the Employment Master who is also unknown. The Employment Master, in consultation with a Tibetan outsourcing firm, actually extends a job offer to the selected candidate. Then an extensive barrage of security, intelligence, and behavioral tests are administered. Compared to our process, the selection of a new Pope may seem haphazard and rushed.

Everyone on the Management Quintet knew this was a critical hire. As the head of Domestic Secrets, Mr. X had consolidated multiple departments and hundreds of employees into a single unit—which blindly followed his every order without question. His replacement would be granted similar powers, so only the best of the best were considered. We were told these candidates far exceeded the requirements of the race, yet everyone backed a different horse.

There was real tension in the air because the soul of the company was at stake. If Simply Secrets didn't get this just right, employees might question their leadership ability. After all, no one at this level had ever resigned before, and Mr. X's departure still reverberated throughout the workforce. If one left, then ten, and then a hundred—where would it stop? Had the floodgates been opened, irreversibly draining our great organization of all its human capital?

---

2 J. Hobart Matheson, Esq. Born 1947, Teaneck, NJ.

A Second Chance

Despite everything, we must admit that Mr. X was really quite a guy. Direct, innovative, and self assured, he brought a strong personality and competitive spirit to all things. That's why Domestic Secrets was consistently the most profitable division under Mr. X's tenure. Of course, there were detractors: Some considered him brash, egocentric, and flamboyant. Perhaps his success just tended to rub colleagues the wrong way. Mr. X was not a team player, and he seemed unwilling to conform to traditional business practices.

"They brought me here to shake things up," Mr. X had said more than once. "I bring this company a new perspective." And he did shake things up, often questioning his superiors, publicly criticizing business decisions, and rewriting strategy and policy to suit his needs.

The COO once whispered to me sarcastically, "It's a wonder we had any success before Mr. X showed up."

As you may have noticed in the description of the Secret Session, there was no mention of the staff of Human Resources being involved in this process. We have HR personnel, of course. They do wonderful things for us, keep us out of trouble, manage our administrative stuff like payroll and comp, and so on. But the

Executive Board would not suffer their simplistic jingles when it came to replacing Mr. X. There was no time to endure a lecture on the benefits of "diversity of thought" or any other New Age psychobabble. After all, Mr. X had been endorsed by the HR VP herself—and look how that worked out! No, this time out, we were determined to find someone who would always "fit in" here at Simply Secrets.

The Simply Secrets Culture

I'll let you in on a little secret: The further up the ladder you go here, the more politically savvy, diplomatic, conservative, and socially sophisticated you have to be. That's just the way it is, and everyone knows it. Executives must do more than manage the business; they have to handle clients, earn their trust, and connect with them in a meaningful way. The secrets business turns on trust, and the winners here not only know how to earn it—they can use it to great advantage.

I have here on my desk a sealed internal study, entitled "Success Factors, 1970-2005," which lists the common traits of a whole generation of Simply Secrets achievers. I cannot get into the specifics, but the results are astounding. These men all tend to live in the same or adjacent neighborhoods, as do their colleagues, and their children go to school and play together. They all regularly socialize together with their spouses and junior employees; almost all find their wives within the Simply Secrets family. This makes for a real sense of camaraderie on the job. Many analysts cite a relaxed environment and familial atmosphere when discussing the company's early rapid growth.

Mr. X was an anomaly. Although he had significant experience in the secrets business[3], he did not grow up as part of the Simply Secrets family—nor did he particularly embrace it. According to his exit interview, Mr. X thought the company was "lethargic, insular, and adverse to risk." He believed we had rested on our laurels far too long.

The HR VP, whose name we are withholding[4], was a strong advocate of Mr. X and thought his outside experience would bring new ideas and aggressive innovation. He seemed the right man to embrace a new world of increased competition. Mr. X thought that our days as the default industry leader were coming to an end; other executives thought we were going through a temporary downturn. Because Simply Secrets was not attracting many new customers, we hoped that Mr. X could reinvigorate our sales efforts.

---

[3] Covert government operations: Somalia, 1993; Libya, 1996; Florida, 2000.

[4] Polly Peoples, PhD. Born 1952, Sausalito, CA.

As time went on, many employees began to blame Mr. X for all the company's ills. While his division continued to prosper and profit, others did not. Mr. X seemed to be gaining market share by taking it from other parts of the Simply Secrets empire. This kind of irrational success caused a great deal of internal discontent, but Mr. X could have survived—if not for the infamous Memorial Day BBQ.

Held annually at the President's sprawling ranch compound, the barbecue picnic was a time honored tradition at Simply Secrets. Though unspoken, everyone was expected to attend. Mr. X did not show. By the cocktail hour, there were audible rumblings among the partygoers: Where was Mr. X? What a show of disrespect!

The CEO, Chairman of the Board, and the President loudly bemoaned Mr. X's absence which, in turn, became a rant about his entire work style. When it became obvious that no one would spring to Mr. X's defense, the other executives followed suit. Before the first batch of brisket was pulled from the grill, Mr. X had been informally excluded, bypassed, undercut, marginalized, and discounted.

Back in the office, this shift was immediately apparent. Mr. X might as well have been invisible, and it began to take its toll on him. The department's numbers lagged. His workers took long vacations. Mr. X began suffering migraine headaches; he eventually tried counseling two and three days a week—all to no avail. For the good of the company and his mental health, he decided to resign.

That was six months ago, but his complicated legacy remains. Mr. X created a few new products that were successful with customers, but hated by the Simply Secrets staff. They thought these products were fads, beneath the dignity of our fair company. One of the most controversial of these products was the "Daily Secret" program.

On the surface, the "Daily Secret" seems to be a subversion of our mission statement. Instead of protecting a secret, we would offer it (anonymously) to a select group of customers for a small fee.[5] Elite clients in the Domestics Secrets division are entitled to browse through the sanitized secrets of other elite clients, selecting one per day for their reading enjoyment. Mr. X thought that our elite clients wanted to find new ways to spice up their lives. In addition, if your secret is voted best of the month by elite users, then you win free service upgrades, cash prizes, and travel vouchers (some blackouts apply).

---

[5] Simply Secrets does not publicly disclose pricing information, but this service costs $4,275 per month.

The old timers thought the program was a risk and I personally expected our customers to revolt. We were certain that our more sophisticated clients would actually be able to identify the secret they were peering in on. Mr. X allayed our fears by making the program completely voluntary; he required each client to sign a waiver, releasing us to disclose certain pieces of low-threshold data. To our great surprise, 72 percent of the eligible users signed up within three weeks.

By giving our clients access to an unlimited repository of naughty secrets, we were increasing the likelihood that more secrets would be created anew. Thus, it was a self-fulfilling business model. But the success of the program only served to infuriate Mr. X's adversaries even more.

A Very Serious Business

On June 3, at 10:00 a.m., the Executive Board members made their way toward the Chamber of Silence. There are certain security protocols in place to moderate access to the facility, which may or may not include fingerprint analysis, retinal scanning, voice recognition, electronic nerve stimulation, and urinalysis. Rumors of our "Tickle-Scan" technology have been wildly off the mark; full-bore Tickle Scanning will not be commercially available until 2008.

They were all in the Chamber by 11:30 a.m.[6] The Chairman of the Executive Board, known to us as "Mr. Power," called the meeting to order.

"As you all know," he said, clearing his throat, "Mr. X's premature departure has caught us with our pants down again." Power looked at Ms. Peoples, the HR director and only woman in the room, and visibly blushed.

"Excuse my language," he said, continuing. "It's no secret that I consider the tenure of Mr. X to be a disgrace upon our fine organization. And I don't care how much money he made for us. Mr. X was a major disappointment. His inability to play ball like the rest of us hurt morale and productivity. I would be happy if he were the last of our so-called social experiments. Our new director has to fit in, hit the ground running, rally the culture, and make our customers more comfortable. He . . ."

"Or she," Ms. Peoples interrupted.

"Yes," Power whimpered, "or she. He or she has to be darn good! Now, we have the Management Quintet report here. What do you think of it, Ms. Peoples?"

---

[6]The remainder of this narrative has been reconstructed from archival sources, careless whispers, and company scuttlebutt. What happens in the Chamber of Silence, stays in the Chamber of Silence.

Power looked at her as she shuffled through the candidate portfolios. "Well," she said slowly, "they're all pretty good, but these two candidates really caught my eye." She passed two pieces of paper across the table. "They both have the required education, length of experience, proven track record, and executive responsibilities in their favor. They passed our rigorous preliminary testing procedures with exceptional scores, their references check out, and both have similar experience in the secrets industry. And," she trailed off.

"And what?" asked the Chairman.

"And they're both external candidates. One of them had never even heard of us."

Ms. Peoples, HR VP,
Simply Secrets, Inc.

 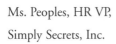

Chapter 3

Prescribed Passages

Mr. Passage had been a quiet observer until now, but suddenly he exploded in anger: "Are you kidding? That's not the way it's supposed to work. Before you get the director's job, you're supposed to work your way up through the ranks. First, you're a low level manager. You cover a single division, then another, and then, if you're doing well, a third. Then you make senior management. That's the Simply Secrets way!"

"But these two candidates . . ." Ms. Peoples sputtered.

"Just look at Mr. X," Mr. Passage continued, interrupting her. "He was an external candidate, too. Oh, how we all got burned by that one! He didn't understand our culture, our customs, or our way of doing business. You can't just drop someone into this company at a high level and expect them to survive."

All eyes were on Ms. Peoples as she slumped in her chair. "I hate to exclude qualified people for any reason," she said. "It doesn't seem right."

The Chairman chimed in: "That's why we established the career path. It's the only way to learn the subtle nuances of our business, to pick up on the tricks of the trade. Each step along the way," he said, gathering his thoughts, "our people are groomed for leadership. Those who don't have what it takes eventually maroon themselves in middle management."

"Not that there's anything wrong with that," Mr. Passage said.

"Oh no," the Chairman responded, "not at all. They may become fine associates, but those who follow the process are better prepared to assume leadership. They've passed key tests along the way."

The Chairman's words echoed through the Chamber, and there was a long pause before anyone spoke. "Why did we hire Mr. X?" someone asked.

"We wanted fresh blood; we wanted someone to shake things up," Ms. Peoples said.

"And then some," said the Chairman. "I remember how vigorously you endorsed him, Ms. Peoples. He was smart and savvy; he had parallel experiences on the outside. He had a scintillating set of core skills. I've heard that HR mumbo-jumbo for years. But there's no substitute for the process: paying your dues and getting your ticket punched. We get to know them through time, and they get to know us. This logical progression is time-tested."

"It's how we all got here," said Mr. Passage.

"Not *all* of us," someone whispered quietly.

"No," said Ms. Peoples. "I was once an outsider here, too. And some days it seems like I still am."

"This is your home, too," Mr. Passage said. "And I would think, after the Mr. X fiasco, that you would be more eager to protect it."

Ms. Peoples calmly stared Mr. Passage down. "You know as well as I do," she said, "that we're growing too quickly to push all of our associates through this sacred pathway of yours. Maybe that kind of thinking worked when we were smaller, but things change, for better or worse."

"It's better for our competitors," the Chairman said, "and worse for us. How are they able to recruit junior managers and place them in senior jobs so quickly? Why does it take our associates so long to get with the program?"

"Either we have to ease up on the requirements," Ms. Peoples shot back, "or you have to look to the outside. You can't have it both ways."

"Do you mean to tell us," Mr. Passage asked, "that there are no internal candidates who meet our criteria?"

"Oh, sure," Ms. Peoples said, laughing. "They may have been here fifteen years or so, and been passed over for promotion a dozen times. They've been, in your words, *marooned* in middle management."

"Not that there's anything wrong with that."

On the Record: Prescribed Passages

"Before you get the director's job, you're supposed to work your way up through the ranks. First, you're a low level manager. You cover a single division, then another, and then, if you're doing well, a third. Then you make senior management. That's the Simply Secrets way!" —Mr. Passage

As Mr. Passage explained, this Fit Factor paves a defined path to success. Do you fit in based on your willingness to follow in the footsteps of those before you, without deviating from traditional expectations? In some jobs, there is no fast track to success. Moving up the ranks requires fulfilling certain rites of passage— paying your dues and earning that partnership, tenured position, or seat at the Executive Roundtable. Often, such jobs entail years of grueling hours and low pay, but the carrot at the end of the stick is wealth, prestige, choice appointments, special schedules, job security, and so on. Consider these scenarios:

- Interns at a prestigious law firm work for free, earning resume "points" that count toward a future partner-track position.
- Young professionals vie for the opportunity to shadow senior executives at a large company, a required rite of passage for leaders in the industry.
- Teachers with newly minted Ph.D.'s toil for years at small, out-of-the-way colleges, making little money, biding their time until they're eligible for tenure.
- Young doctors go into debt, paying their way through several required years of medical school and internships, gaining the degrees and experience necessary to pull down a six-figure salary.

- Television news anchors move from small- and mid-market stations to larger markets to prove their ability to connect with larger audiences.
- Senior leaders know that they will have to relocate to another city or country to round out their portfolio.

Prescribed Passages: Finding Your Fit

What You Need to Know about Yourself

Every company has a prescribed way in and up. For most established companies the pathways are obvious and non-negotiable; but for some, especially in new industries, it can be much more challenging to discover the prescribed passageway to success. It's important for you to determine whether you're the kind of person who feels most comfortable in places that push you down a clear career track. Do you take pride in being part of a profession with longstanding traditions and clear expectations, where loyalty and long term employment really pay off? Or do you fit best in an organization with more mobility, flexibility, and change, less bound by seniority and tradition?

What You Need to Know about the Company

- Is there a clear pathway of progress up the leadership ladder?

- How long are you expected to remain in a job?

- What's too long to stay in a job before you're seen as "marooned?"

- Are there some leaders or departments you must work with in order to be seen as "legitimate?"

- Is working in multiple locations important, possibly requiring you to relocate?

- Can you enter into the organization from another company as long as the level is appropriate? Is it possible to gain "insider status?"

- Are rotations to departments and areas outside of your expertise important or viewed as a detour?

- Is there any evidence that anyone with your identity makeup (race, gender, age, religion, accent, marital or parental status) has successfully made the passage to senior levels? Do people get to the end of their prescribed passage and feel victorious and proud, or broken and hazed?

Fit In!

Chapter 4

Powerful Passion

"Let's shift the discussion a bit," said the Chairman. "I think there were other problems with Mr. X. He tended to be a 9-to-5 type, didn't he?"

"I always saw him racing to the parking lot at five o'clock," someone said.

"He was probably heading to his daughter's soccer practice," Ms. Peoples said curtly. "We say we value work-life balance, gentlemen. Why should we criticize him for being a good father?"

"All that work-life balance stuff," the Chairman said, "that's fine for a manager but not for a director. What kind of example does that set? He had half of his direct reports job-sharing, telecommuting, putting in flextime, and God knows what else."[1]

"I see," Ms. Peoples seethed.

"When you work at this level," Mr. Passion said, "you have to be 100 percent dedicated. VIP clients could call after five on any given day. You have to be available to answer their secret questions. I love this job so much," Passion said, laughing, "the cleaning people have to ask me to leave at night."

Mr. Passion was known for his maniacal dedication. He would walk five miles to the office if his car broke down. He often used personal money to buy supplies as they were needed. He preferred to sleep in his rental car than spend the company's cash at a five-star hotel.

"Then I go home," he continued, "and answer e-mail after my children go to sleep. It's a matter of drive, hunger, focus, and dedication. Mr. X could very well have been here today if he'd taken the offer to run our European office. But he couldn't

---

[1] Again, we must stress that this conversation is reconstructed. I am sure the Chairman would never say anything like this.

relocate because of his wife," Passion said. "So we all knew who wore the pants in that family."[2]

Committee members snickered like they were laughing at a dirty joke.

"That's out of line," Ms. Peoples objected.

"Look," the Chairman said, quieting the room, "you can't be successful in this company if you're not willing to make sacrifices. That's all there is to it."

On the Record: Powerful Passion

"I love this job so much, the cleaning people have to ask me to leave at night." —Mr. Passion

This Fit Factor requires determination and dedication. You fit in based on how hard you work, how much you care about the company, how far you're willing to go to succeed. In some jobs, doing a good job is not enough. The valued employees are those who demonstrate extreme loyalty, enthusiasm, and a willingness

---

2 We have independently confirmed that Mrs. X does indeed wear slacks, jeans, and Capri pants.

to make personal sacrifices on behalf of the company. Though the workday may technically last from 9:00 a.m. to 5:00 p.m., those with Powerful Passion will be at their desks from sunup to long after sundown, diligently putting in extra, unpaid hours. They expect to reap future rewards. Consider these scenarios:

- A stellar employee with young children asks for a flexible schedule and reduced hours—and finds herself on the "Mommy Track."
- Working after hours and on weekends is a badge of honor for a mission oriented not-for-profit.
- Community-service activities, mentoring programs, and company social events are only "optional" if you don't want to move up.
- A mid-level manager moves his/her family several times to take unwanted assignments, sending the message that they're willing to go anywhere or do anything to get ahead.
- A respected employee is counseled to volunteer for committees and informal work groups to demonstrate dedication.

Powerful Passion: Finding Your Fit

What You Need to Know about Yourself

In today's work world of reduced staffs, 24/7 technologies, and increased competition, dedication is a requirement. The challenge is that companies send mixed messages about work-life balance and family-first policies. On the one hand, these polices are established and on the formal books; but in some large organizations, good luck trying to use them!

- Are you the kind of person who will actually try to use these systems? Or do you feel most comfortable in jobs that fire you up, where your passion and dedication are understood, appreciated, and rewarded?

- Do you take pride in your ability to go the extra mile and contribute to a winning team? Or do you require more balance and moderation in your life?

- Do you work to live, or do you live to work?

- Do you see your work as a mission that requires personal sacrifice?

- Where are you in your personal life now?
- Where will you be in a few years—married, raising a family, caring for aging relatives?

Think ahead so you're not marooned later, trying to meet informal requirements that your life will not allow.

What You Need to Know about the Company

- What's the informal expectation for the length of a typical work day?
- Do employees rush back after children are born?
- Do people feel obligated to take Blackberries and laptops on vacation?
- How many times do employees need to relocate in order to advance?
- Do employees have to volunteer for extra projects and task teams to get face-time and exposure?
- Are you expected to participate in all of the social events?
- Does the organization have a history of allowing alternative work choices like telecommuting, job sharing, and flex time?
- Are they tolerant of issues related to parenting, like sickness, school events, and so forth?
- Do you always have to look busy?

Chapter 5

Physical Package

Mr. Package, the Senior Managing Director of Facilities, looked up from his seat at the far end of the conference table. His manicured fingers silently fingered the tip of a Mont Blanc pen. He wore a pinstripe blue suit and gold wire frame eyeglasses. His teeth flashed as he spoke.

"As long as we're speaking candidly," Package said, "I had a few clients call me about Mr. X. It seems he did not instill great confidence in people from the very first impression."

"What do you mean?" asked the Chairman.

"Frankly, sir, the man was only five-foot-five in his dress shoes, and that kind of thing can work against you. You're constantly on the defensive, looking up, trying to see what others are doing. You seem hesitant and unsure—exactly the opposite of what a Secret Keeper should be. There is a look we used to cultivate here. A large, athletic, strong, commanding physical stature seems to make our clients feel at ease."

"Oh, for the love of God," said Ms. Peoples. "What if one of the final candidates is a woman? Especially a petite, feminine, attractive woman; do you think that would work?"

"Really?" asked the Chairman, perking up.

"She is every bit as qualified as the male candidate in every way. She began her career at one of our competitors[1], where she successfully ran the Domestic Division. But she's been succeeding here at Simply Secrets, in quiet ways, for some time. Should I tell her she's too short?"

All of the committee members looked around at each other nervously. They all knew the code, when to avoid something they didn't want to open up. No one wanted to get in the middle of this one with Ms. Peoples.

---

[1] Mum's The Word, Inc.

"Don't get cute," Mr. Package finally said. "We are all speaking frankly here about the reality of business. Even if our words are a little harsh, it shouldn't negate the truth behind them. Ours is a soft business, and real dollars depend on the impressions we make."

"Are you honestly trying to say," Ms. Peoples asked, "that a short person cannot keep a secret as well as a tall person?"

"Not exactly," the Chairman shouted. "But a person with more stature instills a feeling of safety with our clients, and that's important. It pays our salaries."

"Besides," Package added, "our clients would never be comfortable telling their secrets to a woman. You might as well publish them in *People* magazine!"

Silence filled the room—uncomfortable, penetrating, and nerve-racking silence. Everyone wanted to see how Ms. Peoples would react.

But Mr. Package didn't give her a chance to reload. "Polly," he said, "size does matter. Let's face it. If you were walking alone through a parking lot at night, would you feel more threatened by a small man or a large man?"

"That's a stunning analogy," said Ms. Peoples, dripping with sarcasm.

"Whatever. It just proves my point, doesn't it? Our first reading, our first impression, our first instinct—it counts. There is not time to correct it or improve upon it. The sale is made in an instant, without the benefit of thought and consideration."

Ms. Peoples smiled wanly. "Hmmm," she said, "sounds familiar." She casually picked up a sheaf of papers from the table and clicked her pen. "Let's see here," she said, looking over her notes. "Let's find the tallest candidate left."

The Chairman frowned, and Ms. Peoples thought she had gone too far. But just as she was about to apologize, Mr. Package stepped into the breach. "See if you can find an attractive man," he said. "Strong, dark features."

Everyone in the room looked at him. "Um," he stammered, "I mean a lot of our customers are women. They can't wait to unload a secret."

"Your point?" asked the Chairman.

"Well," Package went on, "perhaps they feel more comfortable dealing with an attractive man. Gets rid of all that catty business that goes on between gals."

"Catty business?" Ms. Peoples repeated. "Why don't you tell this 'gal' what you mean by that?"

"It's not just me," said Package. "There's data indicating that they like talking to a good looking guy. You know, the strong and silent type. Someone with a lean build, dreamy eyes, strong hands . . ."

The Chairman cut him off, raising an eyebrow. "Let's stay on topic, Mr. Package."

Package sat down, avoiding the stares. "Look," he said, "our women do all right. They can bring in accounts. But it takes them twice as long to close the sale. We've all seen the transcripts[2]; the conversation wanders this way and that, blah blah blah. A man in the same position could bring in twice the secrets."

"So, you're not saying we should discontinue the use of female salespeople?" asked Ms. Peoples.

"Not at all," Package said. "As long as they're smokin' hot."

With that Ms. Peoples took one of the dossiers and removed it from the Still Under Consideration stack. Now they were down to only two candidates.

---

2 Simply Secrets, Inc. denies all knowledge of such transcripts. Mr. Package was speaking hypothetically.

On the Record: Physical Package

"There is a look we used to cultivate here. A large, athletic, strong, commanding physical stature seems to make our clients feel at ease." —Mr. Package

As Mr. Package described, this Fit Factor focuses on appearances, tying your success to features such as beauty, physical fitness, skin color, attire, grooming, and size. In some jobs, employees face professional, social, or corporate expectations about "the right look." Sometimes these expectations are clearly stated and understood—modeling, professional athletes, dancers—but often there are unspoken company or departmental standards in play also. Consider these scenarios:

- A clothing company wants to project a desirable image for its targeted demographic (translation: it wants all its salespeople to look young, attractive, slim, and "middle-American").

- A technology company prides itself on thinking outside the box (translation: star employees appear creative, brainy, and unencumbered by traditional office attire).

- A nonprofit considers itself edgy, liberal, and politically courageous (translation: it tends to hire employees who advertise their ethnic or cultural identity through clothing, grooming, and personal style).
- A PR firm is seeking high-profile, high-paying clients (translation: the firm's "movers and shakers" wear designer suits, expensive jewelry, shoes, and other accessories).
- A hotel chain prides itself on a clean-cut "all American look" (translation: the company hires people whom they consider to be well groomed with short hair, a great smile).

Physical Package: Finding Your Fit

What You Need to Know about Yourself

Physical Package is one of the more complicated Fit Factors to discuss because it lends itself to violations of equal employment, civil rights, and discrimination laws. Nevertheless, companies still reinforce their package standard by screening people in or out in subtle ways. It is rare to get direct feedback in this area. Your antennae have to be pretty sharp to pick up on this Fit Factor at work.

- Do you prefer to be in jobs where you feel valued for your appearance, cultural identity, and/or personal style, where your physical package is viewed as an asset? Or would you prefer to be in a job where all of the above is ignored?
- Do you take pride in looking the part, whether that means conforming to traditional, conservative societal norms, or rejecting them to appear more cool and stylish?
- Would you prefer to be in an environment where there is a wide range of acceptable packages, where you'll be well within the range of acceptable physical appearance?

What You Need to Know about the Company

- How much of a premium does current leadership place on appearance?
- How does the company use customer preferences as a rationale for the right look?
- What is the company's definition of its corporate image?
- How does the company link professionalism and physical appearances?
- How does the company cater to employees who project desirable physical attributes, such as size, stature, etc.?
- Are there any noticeable fitness norms?
- Have there been any discrimination suits filed, related to any of your identity factors such as race, gender, age, weight?

Chapter 6

Public Relations

Mr. Press, the Communications Commissar, just had to chime in. "I'd like to go back to something," he said. "I really believe in promoting from within, because it's demoralizing for our people to see us go outside for these kinds of opportunities. It sends the wrong signal. I wonder if we shouldn't revise the criteria to allow us to search for an internal candidate who has a little less experience."

"Within reason," Ms. Peoples said.

"Perhaps we're too rigid," Press continued. "Maybe it doesn't take twenty years of experience to make a good director. It certainly didn't take that long for us to rise through the ranks."

The Chairman cleared his throat. The room fell eerily silent. From far off, way beyond the sealed confines of the Chamber of Silence, Press swore he could hear a train whistle.

"What I mean is," Press said, "we had to learn on the job. But the best colleges now offer degree programs in secrets management. These kids are coming in much more prepared." He looked at a list of names laid before him on the table. "For example," he said, pointing down, "what about this person I've been hearing about. I think his name is Potter."

"Perry Potter," said Ms. Peoples without looking up.

"Yes, well, I've heard that he works magic. A real mover and shaker. Been on quite a few important projects, exposed to three divisions, and so forth. Didn't he also lead a task force on anti-identity-theft software?"

"Heard he did a bang-up job on that," said the Chairman.

"He's brought in over a million dollars this year," someone said.

"Here, here," said a voice in back.

"That Potter," said another, "he sure walks on water."

"And I'm sure his farts don't smell," said Ms. Peoples.

"That's quite enough," the Chairman shot back, glaring at her.

"Has any of this been validated?" Ms. Peoples asked. "Except, of course, the farts part."

"He didn't make your list, did he, Ms. Peoples?" Mr. Press walked closer to her, sensing his advantage. "I'm not surprised.

Potter is quite highly regarded in the parts of the company that focus on revenue, which you obviously know nothing about."

Ms. Peoples stood, walked over to a side table, and picked up the telephone. "Give me a secure line," she said into the receiver. The others looked around, dumbfounded. Was Ms. Peoples about to resign? Was she making arrangements to pick up her personal effects?

Ms. Peoples put her hand over the receiver, addressing the men in the Chamber: "Give me fifteen minutes, gentlemen, and we will have a full dossier on Mr. Potter. We can't let someone with such a good reputation be overlooked." She returned her attention to the phone.

On the Record: Public Relations

"I've heard that he works magic. A real mover and shaker."
—Mr. Press

Reputation is everything, according to this Fit Factor. Do you fit in based on your reputation as a go-getter, your record of past accomplishments, and your aura of industriousness? In some jobs, it's what people say about you that counts. Keep your calendar filled with appointments, your desk piled high with important paperwork, and your phone ringing off the hook. Pretty soon, you'll be known as a hot commodity.

Perceived Performers may be genuinely dedicated, skillful workers who sometimes go through a dry spell due to professional or personal reasons. Or they may be good actors. Either way, acting confident and successful is one of the keys to real success. Consider these scenarios:

- A researcher at a biotechnology firm enjoys a national reputation based entirely on past publications, honors, and achievements.

- A journalist is always on the phone or on the road, tracking down exclusive sources for a story that's perpetually in the works.

- A management consultant has a date book bursting with appointments and is always "squeezing" meetings into her hectic schedule.

- The gung-ho CEO of a troubled company kicks off each employee meeting with a rousing report focusing on recent successes, positive news, and future goals.

- A candidate wins an election, and all of a sudden he is touted by the media as a potential candidate for a higher office.

- An actor is in the news several weeks before the release of her next project to generate buzz.

- A junior employee attends events where higher ups will be in order to be seen and to network with the right people.

- A manager volunteers to serve on a task force in order to get visibility and name recognition.

Public Relations: Finding Your Fit

What You Need to Know about Yourself

Statements such as, "There is no such thing as bad publicity" and, "Just spell my name right" may be a bit of a simplification for the business world; but image, aura, and reputation are subtle elements of corporate success. In some organizations the burden is on you to market yourself and let people know about the good work you've been doing. In other organizations, too much self-promotion can sink a career. It's important to use your radar to understand the organization from this perspective so you'll know how to fit in.

How comfortable are you promoting yourself? Some people are by nature more introverted and shy, and find it painfully uncomfortable to take the spotlight.

- Are you the kind of person who was told as a young child not to brag about yourself or toot your own horn?
- Are there identity issues related to your culture that affect how acceptable it is for you to shine over the team? Or are you ready, willing, and able to promote your success and minimize your shortcomings?
- Do you feel most comfortable in jobs where you enjoy an image as a top performer?
- Do you take pride in your professionalism and your ability to rise above failures with a winning attitude?

What You Need to Know about the Company

- Do advancement opportunities work through word of mouth, circumventing the formal posting rules?
- Are words like "face time," "exposure," and "positioning" used regularly?
- Do employees jockey for opportunities to make public presentations to important groups?
- Does the organization have elephant memory for mistakes and failed risks?
- Do employees talk more about individual accomplishments or team victories?
- Are there many or only a few key people to impress or be known by?
- Do you need allies spreading the good word about you throughout the organization?
- Is there a formal feedback and performance appraisal system that is taken seriously?
- Are there opportunities for employees or team members to recognize people "in the trenches" for a job well done?

Chapter 7

Proper Pursuits

Lunch was brought in: platters piled high with fresh sushi, roast beef sandwiches on thick rye bread, a pungent Caesar salad. Some ate quickly, standing, trying vainly with their free hand to find a cell phone signal in the Chamber. Mr. Pursuit, who had shaved his head bald at the first sign of hair loss, walked back to his place at the table. He nibbled at his salad. The bright light shone off his buffed and polished head. "Tasty," he said to no one in particular.

The Chairman agreed and the two men locked eyes. They had been friends and colleagues for twenty years.

"Hobie[1]," Pursuit said, "I think we need someone special."
A couple of chewers looked up, surprised to hear the Chairman's
name spoken aloud.

"What do you mean?" the Chairman asked.

"We need someone who enjoys our pastimes. Mr. X was
always a square peg in a round hole around here. He had ability,
sure, but there's more to success than that. You have to have something in common with your co-workers, a shared sense of mission
and purpose."

"Don't forget," Ms. Peoples said, sipping her soda, "a love
of golf."

"You know," Pursuit continued, "it's really hard to come into
a new business and fit in when you don't have anything in common
with the people around you. Mr. X was the odd man out. He never
bought Girl Scout cookies. He never played Secret Santa."

"He was Jewish[2]," Ms. Peoples said.

"Maybe he should have played a little golf now and then,"
Pursuit said. "He would have made more friends."

"Simply Secrets has a long history of helping underprivi-
leged youth," said Mr. Passion passionately. "It's called the
Clandestine Cares program. You all know it. Well, we volunteer,
we tutor, we work nights and weekends with those kids. And

---

[1] See footnote 2 below.

[2] Simply Secrets, Inc. is an equal opportunity employer.

  Fit In!

every time I asked Mr. X to pitch in, he came up with some excuse: 'I'm going out of town,' he'd say, or 'I've got a commitment' or 'One of my kids is graduating from something.' What about these kids? It's like he didn't give a hoot."

"He never got our jokes," Pursuit said, sadly. "We used to play little tricks on each other, just for fun, and he was always so offended. One time, we made out this pink slip and delivered it to his desk. It was very official-looking."

"You did what?" Ms. Peoples yelled.

"Oh yeah, it was just like the real thing. So we're watching him react, waiting to see the broad smile and hear him break out in laughter, and he just gets this weird look on his face. Starts calling his wife and crying on the phone. What a wet blanket!"

"Unbelievable," Ms. Peoples said, shaking her head.

"No," Mr. Passion said sternly, "I'll tell you what's unbelievable. He actually complained to the Chairman about our Clandestine Cares. He wanted us to divide our time and our energy among several different charities and causes. Didn't he know that nothing gets done that way? You have to pursue a single goal, with single-minded purpose. You have to drive towards the greatest reward."

"He did come to me," said the Chairman. "In confidence, I'll tell you that, but nothing more."

"He openly questioned my integrity," Passion said. "Is it my fault that my brother-in-law runs the Clandestine Cares program? Sure, he takes a modest stipend from the fund.[3] So what? Does that fact help the kids any less?"

"Certainly not," said the Chairman, filling the awkward silence. "We help the kids and that's what matters. It fosters a real sense of camaraderie here. Getting ahead doesn't always mean you have to be right; it means you have to get along. Mr. X, I'm afraid, never learned that lesson."

On the Record: Proper Pursuits

"We need someone who enjoys our pastimes. Mr. X was always a square peg in a round hole around here. He had ability, sure, but there's more to success than that. You have to have something in common with your co-workers, a shared sense of mission and purpose." —Mr. Pursuit

When this Fit Factor comes into play, what you do after hours matters as much as what you do at the office. Company acceptance at senior levels is based on the neighborhood where you live, the church you attend, and the recreational activities you enjoy. In some jobs, the doorway to success opens when you play

---

[3] This practice has since been discontinued.

the right games, socialize in the right venues, or seek a lifestyle that mirrors that of key managers and executives. Lucrative deals may be made on the golf course; employees may brush elbows with higher-ups in upscale social outings. There may also be an unspoken desire to extend the company's brand and image through the lifestyles of its employees.

Consider these scenarios:

- At a Manhattan investment firm, the power brokers gather at swanky Wall Street bars and restaurants after hours.

- At an outdoor equipment company, employees spend every Monday morning talking about where they biked, hiked, or kayaked during the past weekend.

- At the Midwest regional office of a large communications company, everyone goes to church on Sundays—and we do mean everyone.

- The CEO of a small company is passionate about baseball, so he invites fellow devotees to join him at night and weekend games.

- A team at a high tech company all share a passion for extreme sports and regularly get together after work and on the weekends.

- Executives at a successful advertising firm regularly golf with VIP clients.

Proper Pursuits:
Finding Your Fit

What You Need to Know about Yourself

Proper Pursuits is another one of the Fit Factors, like Physical Package, that has a customer focus as well as an informal internal organizational focus. Many businesses still woo potential and current customers with tickets to complementary sports and cultural outings.

In addition, some companies build camaraderie and team sprit through participation in regular group activities, the specific activity depending on the organization. Many want-to-be managers and executives will adopt the sport of choice in order to fit in.

- How comfortable do you feel in jobs where your lifestyle is celebrated and your after-hours activities are shared with those you work with?
- Do you take pride in your personal passions and feel fortunate to have a job where work and "real life" go hand in hand?
- How comfortable are you mixing business and pleasure with clients and co-workers?

What You Need to Know about the Company

- Is there a sport or activity of choice? Is it one that you're comfortable with?
- Are decisions about important business issues discussed at social occasions and company outings?
- Are those activities biased in ways that create barriers for identity groups that you are a member of?
- Do the personal pursuits require a lot of time after work that create work-life balance issues that will overcomplicate your life?
- Is there an additional cost to participating in such events that will make it difficult for you financially?

Chapter 8

Powerful Patronage

The Chamber suddenly went dim. A red light, anchored to the ceiling, began to pulse rapidly. Everyone heard a mechanical whoosh as the doors locked and bolted into place. A gargantuan bubble descended swiftly from the darkness, encapsulating the table, chairs, and everyone in the room. Within fifteen seconds, they were all under glass, breathing canned oxygen.

The Committee members appeared more confused than frightened. They knew better than to speak a word. Soon the flat-panel monitors would also descend, illuminating the glass cocoon with a blue glow, dispensing news and procedural instructions. A man's face flickered across the screens. The Simply Secrets fanfare played in the background as the face began to speak.

"Gentlemen," he said. Then he seemed to adjust to the darkness and really look around the room. "And lady."

Ms. Peoples wondered, as the rest of them did, if he could really see her. She watched his eyes closely, but was distracted by the appearance of text on the screen: "Mr. Patronage, CEO."

He looked like a man in his fifties, a former athlete just now giving up on the physical tests of youth. He was tanned and trim, and his teeth shone pearly white. It was the first time any of them—including the Chairman—had ever seen his face. It was a well-guarded secret in a company built on secrets. For security purposes, he had no official record of employment. He was not on any e-mail list. He never attended shareholder meetings.[1]

"Don't be alarmed," he said. "This is not an emergency. I wish there was an easier way to get in touch with you all, but you know how strict our policies are." The Committee members mumbled their agreement. "You probably thought we had a secret escape, or worse: Total Archive Meltdown." Now there was nervous laughter.

---

[1] Rumor has it that the CEO was paid through intermediaries, via courier, and in cash. This disclosure should in no way constitute an endorsement of this policy. Remember, the IRS has its secrets, too.

  Fit In!

"The last time we had one of those," Patronage continued, "I had to lock everything down, gas the building into sleep, sniff out the problem, blitz the repair, cover our tracks, and zap everyone's memory[2] before they came to."

"I don't remember that," said the Chairman.

"Exactly," said the CEO. "Anyway, I'm here today to put in my recommendation for the Director of Domestic Secrets." There was an audible gasp from the back of the room. "I've been tracking the career of someone for quite some time now. He's working in the Celebrity Secrets Division, but don't let that fool you. He's quite an up-and-comer, based on all of the feedback I've received. He knows the company inside and out. I've been quiet about my involvement with his career until now because," Patronage paused, "well, I wanted to make sure he could cut the mustard on his own."

"Who do you have in mind?" Ms. Peoples asked.

"I heard some of you discussing it earlier," Patronage said. "We want someone from the Simply Secrets family, right? Well, this candidate is all that and more. He's my nephew."

---

[2] The Simply Secrets Memo-Raser™. Available June 2007.

On the Record:
Powerful Patronage

"I've been quiet about my involvement with his career until now because," Patronage paused, *"well, I wanted to make sure he could cut the mustard on his own."*
—The Simply Secrets CEO

It's all about who you know, according to this Fit Factor. Do you fit in based on your connections to the company elite? In some jobs, success depends on your relationships with mentors, influential leaders, and others on the inside track. Getting ahead may require politicking behind the scenes, impressing key people, and cultivating a reputation as "a player." In some professions (such as politics), the importance of Powerful Patronage is openly acknowledged.

Consider these scenarios:

- All federal job openings must officially be posted to the public, but many are created with specific, internal candidates in mind.

- A foundation awards generous research grants to promising young scientists, but proposals are judged largely by the reputation of their recommenders.

- A coveted senior-level position opens up, but the VP skips internal candidates to hire a colleague from his previous company.
- A company in a male-dominated industry establishes a mentoring program to help women break the glass ceiling, but women who aren't in the program remain stuck in low-paying jobs.

Powerful Patronage: Finding Your Fit

What You Need to Know about Yourself

In most organizations your ability to network and establish relationships with powerful superiors is the key to establishing meaningful mentoring relationships. Companies that make a point of "establishing a level playing field," downplay the importance of Powerful Patronage. Yet they establish mentoring programs, internships, and other avenues that pave the way for well connected individuals. And still atop the "official programs," the unofficial mentoring and string pulling continues.

- How comfortable are you in an organization where someone from above must vouch for you or sponsor you in order for you to gain entry to higher levels?

- How easy will it be for you to establish affinity and connect with higher-ups who may be from another generation or a different cultural identity group?

What You Need to Know about the Company

- Are people chosen to be groomed and moved into choice opportunities from above?
- Are certain jobs earmarked for individuals ahead of time?
- Do people get inside information and warnings from their sponsors and mentors?
- Is there a formal mentoring program?
- Are new hires assigned a contact, buddy, or mentor?
- Have others come into the company from outside or a different department and received ready acceptance and support?
- Are employment decisions made by one person or a committee?

Chapter 9

Potential Performance

Morning faded into afternoon, and then the early evening came, though it was difficult to tell since the Chamber had no windows and there were no clocks on the walls. The Committee had diligently considered the candidacy of the CEO's 27-year-old nephew, eventually rejecting it on logistical grounds. The new Director of Domestic Secrets could not conduct his business via telephone from an underground bunker. He could not, as the CEO suggested, "check in every now and then." And he most certainly could not keep his name and appearance secret.

After the glass dome was raised and the monitors retracted, coffee was brought in. Everyone dutifully indulged. Mr. Potential, dropping five or six teaspoons of sugar into his cup, addressed the group: "Can we dig a little deeper into the talent pool, like Mr. Press suggested, and find someone who has raw talent? Maybe we need someone young, eager, and willing to learn."

"Hmmm," the Chairman mused aloud, "we could use some new blood, some excitement, someone with untainted perspectives."

"Like Mr. X?" asked Ms. Peoples.

"No," the Chairman said, "but I'm sure you must know some younger people who would work their hearts out to have this opportunity. Think of it like the football draft: Some players go bust, sure, but others go to the Hall of Fame. Law firms do this all the time; they recruit the top students from the best law schools. Maybe we've been going at this thing from the wrong angle."

Ms. Peoples looked pleased, but decided to keep her mouth shut. She knew this was the first sensible suggestion she had heard all day, but didn't want to throw her support behind it just yet. There was such a negative vibe in the room towards her; she feared her approval would kill the idea.

CEO Power spoke up: "Just what are you suggesting, sir? How would we groom this person? Who has time for grooming?

We have quarterly goals, half-year goals, and yearly goals. If we don't meet those goals, we're not going to excuse our failure because we were busy 'grooming someone' for another job."

"Our bonuses are tied to financial earnings and based on very clear criteria. Raw talent is nice," Power said, pausing for effect, "but you have to immediately contribute to the bottom line here, or your tenure will be short."

"You're probably right," said Mr. Potential. "I just thought it was worth mentioning."

On the Record:
Potential Performance

"Think of it like the football draft: Some players go bust, sure, but others go to the Hall of Fame." —Mr. Potential

The first ingredient for success is raw talent, according to this Fit Factor. Do you fit in based on your intelligence, your innate abilities, or some past accomplishments? Or is it the depth of your knowledge or skill? At some jobs and stages of careers, it's not what you do, but what you're perceived to be capable of doing. Rumors often fly in this kind of work environment, where so-and-so is reputed to have a sky-high IQ, an extraordinary talent, and it's a short step from there to being seen as the Next

Big Thing. While everyone is supposedly playing by the same rules—and required to meet the same deadlines, performance targets, etc.—Potential Performers sometimes get a free pass.

Consider these scenarios:

- A writer with an acclaimed novel under her belt receives a generous advance for her second book, despite the fact that she hasn't yet written a word.

- A computer scientist at a big technology firm receives a handsome salary and an important title, although his last breakthrough was achieved years ago, when he was still a college student.

- A star college graduate is recruited and given a higher starting salary than those who have ten years on the job.

- A college basketball player is drafted by the NBA and rewarded with a big contract and signing bonus, although he has yet to score a single point at the pro level.

Potential Performance: Finding Your Fit

What You Need to Know about Yourself

Intelligence and innate talent are recognized and applauded in organizations where Potential Performance is a premium. The hot new stars are celebrated for their brilliance, genius, or great skill.

These are environments where leaders like to identify, develop, and shape raw potential. This usually begins at more junior positions, but the glow of being identified early on as the next generation of talent can have a momentous career impact. Often past stars become the coaches and leaders of the new generation because they have the distinguishing credibility to take the lead in shaping others.

Are you a star? Is it acknowledged? Because if you're not already identified as a prodigy or genius, it may be too late to make that miracle happen. How will you do in an organization where you may have been a constant contributor who is recognized for your work product, consistency, or loyalty only to see a "younger model" swoop in whom you must train and prepare to take leadership ahead of you?

What You Need to Know about the Company

- Do new recruits that come from prestigious environments move up the ladder more quickly than others who have worked constantly over the years?
- Does the company invest time and money recruiting from the best schools or wooing the best young stars away from its competitors?

- Do new recruits start in more prestigious jobs than others who begin at the same time?
- Are there fast track programs for those identified as having potential early on? What are the requirements to enter such programs?
- Are there people who share any of your identity factors recognized as being a star or up-and-comer?
- Are there older employees who are passed over in favor of the young guns?

Fit In!

Chapter 10

Personal Presence

There was a knock at the outer vestibule door, and the Chairman's administrative assistant went to answer it. He came back into the room with a stack of files. "Here's the stuff on the new candidates," he said.

"Finally," said Ms. Peoples. "They must have gone deep into the archives for this material." She took the stack of papers, threw open the top envelope, and immediately knew why.

"Ah," she said, looking at a few words. "The CEO's Nephew. Everything is blank. We've already ruled him out."

"Yes," the Chairman agreed. "Who else do you have there?"

"The magical Mr. Perry Potter. This person is a real find," Peoples said, plucking out a file. "Very competent. Gets superior performance ratings in every category." A shadow of a smile crossed her face. "Except one."

"What's that?" asked Mr. Press who was clearly defending his candidate.

"Well," Ms. Peoples said, "it seems our new knight in shining armor is about as dull as a doorknob."

Mr. Press was incredulous. "Perhaps you should investigate more thoroughly," he said. "How can you say he's dull? If you look at his scores, year after year, it can't be all that bad."

"Year one," Peoples said, reading the document, "Needs improvement, very limited communications skills. Year two: Needs improvement, uncomfortable with public speaking, cannot capture an audience during sales presentations. Year three: Poor. Client fell asleep during sales presentation. Year four: Client's dog fell asleep. Need I go on?"

"No," Press said.

Mr. Presence spoke up: "Well, that's that. We cannot have him. You need charisma in this job; it's even more important to your success than physical stature. Our directors have to be high-energy. Our clients and associates literally feed off of that energy.

It's the kind of thing that people are attracted to."

"There are some positives," Ms. Peoples said. "It seems Mr. Solid is very good at assessing client needs and crafting killer proposals. So he struggles with the pizzazz a little. So he's a little shy. There may be more to this guy than I think."

"Not everyone is a raging extrovert like you, Ms. Peoples," Mr. Press said.

"The Director of Domestic Secrets," said the Chairman "has a lot of client contact. He has to woo people, hold their hands, sell them on our services, and convince large groups to utilize our services."

"He's also got to be a motivator," said Mr. Presence. "Mr. Solid doesn't sound like an inspiration. No offense."

"None taken," said Ms. Peoples. "But let's look at the whole picture." She flipped through a few more pages. "He really excels at new product development and technology. Maybe that matters more than being a great people person. He'd be just right to lead systems or strategy projects—especially when his clients are internal, not external."

"So," the Chairman said, "hire Perry Potter for something else."

"I just might," she said.

On the Record: Personal Presence

"Our directors have to be high-energy. Our clients and associates literally feed off of that energy. It's the kind of thing that people are attracted to." —Mr. Presence

Style and charisma are the keys to this Fit Factor. Do you fit in based on your personal charm, your charisma and flair, and your powers of persuasion? At some jobs, your credentials and experiences are less important than your personality. Actors and other celebrities, for example, often rise to prominence based on sex appeal, star quality, likeability, and so forth. But even in less glamorous jobs, a commanding Personal Presence may explain why some employees seem to fly up the company ladder, while others find themselves stuck on the bottom rungs. Consider these scenarios:

- At a technology start-up, the CEO establishes an informal meeting style where all employees are expected to chime in, speak their minds, and prove their mettle.
- A casual, family-style restaurant is renowned (and richly rewarded) for its warmth, hospitality, and friendly staff.

- Smooth operators who project cool confidence move quickly up the ranks at a marketing firm, while less polished peers remain in less powerful roles.
- A politician who has good ideas is overlooked because she lacks "charisma."

Personal Presence: Finding Your Fit

What You Need to Know about Yourself

Here are some questions to ask yourself:

- Do you feel most comfortable in jobs where you can use the power of your personality to impress, persuade, and achieve?
- Do you take pride in your natural ability to seize the day and leverage your wit, charm, and command of the moment?
- Would you describe yourself as a real people person who enjoys taking center stage within teams, with clients or constituents? Or do you prefer to work quietly behind the scenes, letting the quality of your work and the strength of your ideas speak for you?

What You Need to Know about the Company

- Are there a range of styles, such as introverts and extroverts, who gravitate toward the top?
- How important are presentation skills?
- What are the preferred qualities that are seen as effective—humor, command, vocabulary, self-confidence, empathy?
- Are any of the qualities biased against identity groups you belong to?
- Is the company clear about the differences of qualities and competencies, or are they mixed together?
- How does the company give feedback about style and presentation?

Chapter 11

Preferred Pedigree

"Not so fast," said Mr. Pedigree. He was a small man who rarely spoke, but now he rose from his seat with a theatrical flair. "Are we just going to ignore our CEO? I know his nephew is a little wet behind the ears, but he's the product of impeccable upbringing and schooling."

"High schooling," Ms. Peoples said.

Mr. Pedigree continued undaunted. "We've talked all day about finding someone who can quickly grasp our culture, who knows how we do business and will bring stability to the division. We want to send a signal to our people that they have a chance to grow here."

"But we cannot practice blatant nepotism," said the Chairman.

"But there are other candidates, quality men from good families. Maybe they don't have much experience, but they have been groomed for success from birth—schools, fraternities, social clubs, country clubs . . . They've had the kind of experiences that can easily connect with our clients' social background," Pedigree insisted.

"I can't help noticing," Ms. Peoples said, sounding more defeated than angry, "that you keep using the male pronoun. Are we so convinced it has to be a man?"

"I'm speaking frankly," said Mr. Pedigree. "I just think you can throw a well-groomed man into the water and he will swim, they've prepared for that kind of challenge. In my experience, a young man from his background will work harder and devote himself more. He will not let his family down. He believes in upholding that honor."

Ms. Peoples, recovering her rage, rolled her eyes. "I certainly don't want to go against the sacred order," she said, "but I also don't want to come back into this room in a year or two because this guy flamed out."

On the Record:
Preferred Pedigree

"Maybe they don't have much experience, but they have been groomed for success from birth—schools, fraternities, social clubs, country clubs. They've had the kind of experiences that can easily connect with our clients' social background." —Mr. Pedigree

This Fit Factor stresses the importance of your family, social, educational, and professional background. Do you fit in based on your family name, the schools you attended, the clubs or fraternities you joined, the internships or awards you garnered? In some jobs, having the right background matters as much—if not more—than what you've actually accomplished in your career. This was especially true in the past, when many jobs were reserved solely for the upper classes or Ivy League graduates. Today, most companies make an effort to hire and promote people from all walks of life, yet still, Preferred Pedigree is often used as an unofficial yardstick, particularly for senior-level appointments and positions. Consider these scenarios:

- A museum seeks donations from wealthy, socially prominent individuals, so the fundraising department is looking for a director with a social pedigree who can relate to potential patrons.

- A hospital wants its name on the "top ten" list of a national magazine, so its new recruitment effort targets doctors from prestigious medical schools.

- A young Harvard graduate becomes an entrepreneur and hires other Ivy League grads to join her management team.

- A consulting firm woos clients by "wining and dining" them, so only reps with the right background, connections, and social etiquette handle its high-profile accounts.

- A major company reserves certain jobs for the relatives of the founder.

Preferred Pedigree: Finding Your Fit

What You Need to Know about Yourself

Ask youself these questions:

- Do you feel most comfortable in jobs where your background is an asset?
- Are you comfortable using your family background and social milieu as a way to gain entrée and respect?
- Do you want to work in an environment where you and your employer hold certain educational and professional institutions in high esteem?
- Do you want to work with others who come from institutions or families of social prominence?
- Are you an average Joe or Jane who emerged from humble roots—dedicated to hard work?

What You Need to Know about the Company

- Do the executive ranks swell with graduates from certain prestigious schools?
- Do appointments of new leaders land on the society pages of local newspapers?
- Do people who have limited experience parachute into executive jobs because they come from the current political administration or have had media exposure?
- Does it help to have recommendations or connections to the outside with celebrities, recognized experts, and prominent individuals?

Chapter 12

Proper Perspective

"**I** support this one wholeheartedly," said Mr. Perspective, pointing towards a file. "I think he's going to take this company to the next level." Everyone turned towards him, expecting an explanation, but Perspective didn't say anything else. He just sat there smiling.

"Who?" asked Ms. Peoples?

"Perry Potter," Perspective said, passing the file around. "He may not have an electric personality, but we can count on him to hit the ground running. Plus, he's been a big contributor to Clandestine Cares. He'll have the mindset we need to reintegrate the Domestics Division back into the flow of the company. Right now it's terribly isolated because X made enemies. Solid will know how to play ball and be a team player!"

"I thought we had dispensed with Mr. Potter," said the Chairman.

"He's got just enough of everything," Perspective said. "Not too bright, not too dim. Not too aggressive, not too cautious. Not too old, not too young, confident yet not arrogant! It's the law of averages, gentlemen. Perry Potter, on balance, has everything we need."

"And nothing we want," the Chairman said. "Say, who's the number-two man in Domestic Secrets?"

"Deputee, sir."

The men in the room—everyone except the Chairman— looked around nervously. They weren't quite sure where Ms. Peoples was headed, but no one thought to interrupt the conversation.

"And this Deputee," said the Chairman," has been doing a good job?"

"Stellar," said Ms. Peoples. She reached across the table to pick up one of the discarded folders. She flipped it open and read silently for a moment before continuing. "Since Mr. X's departure, productivity is up 5 percent."

"That's astounding!" the Chairman roared.

Ms. Peoples kept reading, but her eyes began to light up. She was clearly enjoying this new turn of events. "That's not all," she said. "Deputee has the department running under budget. It seems Deputee really knows where to trim the fat."

"Ms. Peoples," said the Chairman, "I cannot believe that you did not add Deputee to your candidate list."

"Oh, but I did," Peoples said. "Deputee was not eliminated from consideration until I heard from the people in this room."

"Regardless, this Deputee sounds like a great fit. I say we make an offer. What do you say?"

"I couldn't agree more," said Ms. Peoples.

"Terrific!" yelled the Chairman. "That's settled. Deputee is our man!"

"Well, sir," Peoples said, "you mean, our woman."

"What?" asked the Chairman.

"We're going to hire Ms. Darlene Deputee to run Domestic Secrets. So, technically, we've found our woman."

"Let me get this straight," the Chairman said. "The number-two man isn't a man at all?"

"Yes," said Ms. Peoples.

The Chairman and Ms. Peoples looked at each other for a long time. Neither one moved.

"Let's write it up," said the Chairman. "I'm tired and I want to go home."

"Who's up for a Clandestine Cares softball game?" asked Mr. Passage. "There's still time to get to the park."

"I'm going out of town," someone said, heading out the door.

"I've got a commitment," said another.

"One of my kids is graduating from something," said Ms. Peoples, smiling.

On the Record: Proper Perspectives

"He'll have the mindset we need to reintegrate the Domestics Division back into the flow of the company."
—Mr. Perspective

This Fit Factor establishes "right" and "wrong" opinions for company employees. Do you fit in based on your views on politics, art, science, business, morality, company policy? In some jobs, success depends on your willingness to "toe the company line," rallying around a set of ideas, attitudes, or philosophies. The pressure to conform may come from the company's executives or from other key leaders, simply because they feel strongly about their beliefs. It may also stem from the company's mission or from longstanding traditions established by the organization's founders. Consider these scenarios:

- At a soup kitchen and anti-hunger organization, employees are seen as doing "God's work" by helping the needy.

- At an advertising company, successful account reps are those who believe "the client is always right"—even when the client seems misguided or misinformed.

- At a high-flying Fortune 500 company, profits are always up—even if this requires a little "creative accounting" on the part of financial executives and other employees.

- At an urban high school, teachers are expected to embrace a curriculum and a teaching philosophy that places heavy emphasis on multiculturalism, gender equity, and nontraditional reading material.

Proper Perspectives: Finding Your Fit

What You Need to Know about Yourself

- Do you feel comfortable in jobs where you share certain beliefs, values, and points of view with your colleagues?

- Do you take pride in expressing your opinion and working in an atmosphere where your beliefs are validated?

- Are you an independent thinker, someone who enjoys arguing points until the best conclusion has been reached?

- Will you speak your mind regardless of who it may offend?

What You Need to Know about the Company

- How much dissent is tolerated?

- Are people warned not to raise "sacred cows"?

- Are those who challenge the prevailing norm seen as troublemakers?

- Is it viewed as disloyalty to criticize the company?

- Are decisions easy to reach because there is little debate?

chapter 13

The Fit Scan Epilogue: Ms. Deputee Speaks

Author's Note: This transcript was taken from a digital audio recording, made June 17, 2006, in the office of Dr. Phineas Phit, a certified fit analyst. The sound source has been cleaned up considerably, and the identities of the two speakers authenticated. Simply Secrets is neither legally nor ethically compelled to reveal the reason for this recording, nor are we prepared to confirm or deny its existence.

Darlene Deputee: Good Morning, Doctor. It's a pleasure to meet you.

Phineas Phit: Ah, Ms. Deputee. I've been expecting you. Have a seat.

Deputee: Thanks. I think you know why I'm here.

Phit: They've offered you Domestic Secrets. Ms. Peoples told me.

Deputee: Yes.

Phit: Good show. But you're worried about something, aren't you?

Deputee: How did you know?

Phit: People don't come to see me unless they're worried. You cannot be a certified fit analyst for long without spotting that.

Deputee: How does it work? I mean, what do you do?

Phit: It's very simple, Ms. Deputee. I ask you a few questions. We discuss your attitudes and opinions about work. We also investigate the culture that you're trying to fit into. Once we have that information, we can try to figure out if it's the right place for you.

Deputee: Sounds easy.

Phit: Yes and no. I may ask you to make some very hard choices, and to be perfectly honest about who you are and what you want. If you cannot do that, then you're just wasting our time. It's good that you're here, that you recognize the value of this kind of analysis. So many people—most people, actually—just drift from job to job, unfulfilled, always looking for greener pastures.

Deputee: That's not me, Doctor. This is my dream job.

Phit: OK, let's start there. What makes it so perfect?

Deputee: I have always dreamed of being the first woman to head up a major department, and Domestic Secrets is the crown jewel in the Simply Secrets empire. The business is respected throughout the industry.

Phit: Ah, so you're doing this for the prestige?

Deputee: Well, a little, but I guess it has more to do with my sense of self. I want to prove that a woman can do the job.

Phit: So, you want to be a pioneer?

Deputee: Yes. It's more than that, too. I want to really make some changes from within.

Phit: You want to shift the culture?

Deputee: Yes.

Phit: I see. What if I asked you to rank your reasons for taking the job? I want to see if you can put them in order. Let's start with the top five.

Deputee: OK, first would be the pioneering woman thing. Next, culture shift. Third, prestige. Then, let's see . . . How do I put this?

Phit: Put it bluntly. There's no one else here.

Deputee: OK then, let's make the last two power and money. There, I've said it.

Phit: So, looking at my notes here, we have female empowerment, fostering change, gaining prestige, wielding power, and making money. I want you to remember those five things because I'm going to make you give most of them up.

Deputee: What?

Phit: In due time, Ms. Deputee. Now let's talk about the Simply Secrets culture. How do young women fit in there?

Deputee: It's a bit of an old boys' club. Frankly, Doctor, I'm one of the few women in any position of authority.

Phit: Why are women excluded?

Deputee: They just don't fit into their picture of secret keeping, or salesmanship, or something. They think the clients really only trust a man of stature to make them feel safe and "guard their secrets."

Phit: Women don't live up to a perceived Physical Package of success?

Deputee: Yes, exactly. And then they still hold on to stereotypes about women "gossiping" that may have been partially true at one point in time, but not today.

Phit: And will you be able to change that?

Deputee: Well, I'm just one person, Doctor. I suppose I'll have to deal with it. But I'm used to it really.

Phit: Exactly! Now you see what I'm getting at. That's one thing that you'll have to deal with in the new job. It will annoy you, frustrate you, and perhaps even keep you from doing everything you want to do. But you're willing to live with it?

Deputee: I guess I am. It hasn't bothered me up to this point in my career.

Phit: If it gets rough, do you have a mentor or patron that you can turn to?

Deputee: Mentor? Patron? Me? Well, yes, he's the guy I'm replacing. There are professors and colleagues at old jobs, too.

Phit: No one on the inside then?

Deputee: I was never part of the "in" group.

Phit: So, Simply Secrets grooms people for success? Mostly men, in this case, are brought up through the ranks by a guiding hand?

Deputee: Exactly. But even that wasn't enough for my old boss and he was a man. Mr. X fought them the entire time and ran interference for me. We created new divisions that I ran over the years, but none of the other executives were familiar with my work because I progressed entirely within Domestic Secrets.

Phit: So, that's another thing that you'll have to deal with. Not only do you work solo, without a mentor, but you charted your own pathway and passages through the organization, with the support of your X boss. You are not apt to follow any traditional paths to the top.

Deputee: Not if I can help it.

Phit: You know that may mean that they'll always see you as a little bit of an outsider? But you may be able to connect with them in other ways. Where did most of the executives come from before they were employed by Simply Secrets? Schools, past jobs?

Deputee: That's just it Doc, they mostly grew up in the organization. These men were on the forefront of the Secrets industry. That's why they're so knowledgeable, considered the best in the world. Many of them have never worked anywhere else at all.

Phit: And if my records are clear, you came from a prestigious university program. How do you think they feel about your educational background? Your pedigree? Do you think they're ready for a degreed executive?

Deputee: I doubt it. They go back a long way together. All these guys were busy doing the work while the university types were only theorizing about it. They bonded during the glory days for the industry. They all like the same things, their wives and families all socialize together. Come to think of it, they're less a club and more like a community.

Phit: Hmmm, I'm glad you said that. So you don't share any pastimes or tend to socialize with your co-workers?

Deputee: No.

Phit: Do you think it would help if you did?

Deputee: Help what?

Phit: Your career. Maybe you'd cultivate a mentor during these social occasions, someone who would take an interest in your career.

Deputee: Well, sure. It wouldn't hurt. But I'm not about to convert, or start playing golf. Do you know how boring golf is? Besides I already play the silly Secret Santa game year round!

Phit: I love golf myself, but that's neither here nor there. The point is, you're not willing to try to join the established social circle. You've never shared their passions outside of work, and you're unwilling to start now—no matter what it does to your career.

Deputee: I don't know if I would say that.

Phit: But you did say that, Ms. Deputee. You said it loud and clear. And you should be glad that you did say it, because otherwise you wouldn't think about that compromise or its repercussions.

Deputee: I'm starting to catch on, Doc. What we're doing here, really, is taking a hard look at the company's informal expectations and a hard look at my bottom lines. That way, we can see where the irritations are.

Phit: We call it "the gap," Ms. Deputee: the gap between your ideal work culture and the one that you're actually in—or going into, in this case. If the gap is too large, you will struggle and probably fail to achieve your goals. On the other hand, if you can compromise on a few things, you can narrow the gap, and you may be able to stay and succeed.

Deputee: Interesting. So far, I guess that gap is pretty wide. But I just know I can do this job, and I know that my colleagues think I can do it, too.

Phit: What makes you say that?

Deputee: I've always gotten good reviews, always been the "up and comer," and so on. They've always told me that they expect great things.

Phit: You have tremendous potential.

Deputee: Absolutely.

Phit: That's good news. If they have a strong belief in your potential performance, that can negate so many challenging Fit Factors. That's if they truly value potential. We'll learn more about that as we go on.

Deputee: I like the sound of that.

Phit: Let me ask you another question: Are you famous?

Deputee: Hardly.

Phit: I mean within the organization. Are you a Simply Secrets star?

Deputee: Maybe. I am a little conservative because of my age. I was raised to be respectful of those who are older, and a part of respect is not upstaging them. I only wish more people knew my record. I brought in so much business under Mr. X—business that he often took credit for—and I made great changes to the department. Did you know that our operating revenue nearly doubled during my brief tenure as the second-in-command?

Phit: I didn't know that. But it doesn't matter what I know. It's what the people at Simply Secrets know. They may all assume that Mr. X did the work by himself.

Deputee: Ha! I was the power behind that throne.

Phit: And a lot of good it did you, if no one gives you credit for the results. You have to be able to tell your own story. Your public relations has to be top notch.

Deputee: I just don't like bragging about myself, that's all.

Phit: I understand. It's sometimes uncomfortable to toot your own horn. But are you willing to change that behavior?

Deputee: Yes, I think that's a good idea. I should be more forthcoming about my accomplishments.

Phit: So, that's something you can change in order to succeed. Speaking about being forthcoming, what's the management style of senior executives at Simply Secrets? Outgoing? Reserved? Argumentative? Team oriented? Autocratic?

Deputee: Well, I'd say it's a bit of flair, charm, and persuasiveness mixed in with a little B.S. They fawn over clients. Some of that spills over into how they deal with one another.

Phit: How would you describe your style in relation to that?

Deputee: Well, I'd have to say I'm much more matter of fact. Much more to the point. Much more . . .

Phit: Abrupt?

Deputee: I would describe it as focused and efficient. But I guess I could see how they could see it in that light.

Phit: Are you willing to loosen up a bit? Stretch a little to be more outgoing and effusive? So when you're with them, your presence is not so jarring by contrast?

Deputee: I could try. It's not really who I am. But I wish they would listen to what I say and not how I say it!

Phit: And what about what you're saying, Ms. Deputee? Have all of your new ideas that led to the growth in revenue been well received?

Deputee: Not all of them very well, Doctor. They seem to think my perspectives on the future business environment of the Clandestine Industry are too "trendy." For example, I'm still sitting on the best new product innovation yet, the Forgiveness Program. My research proves that people would be willing to pay for forgiveness along with burying the secret. Mr. X fought a big battle over it shortly before he resigned. The others on the executive team thought it was sacrilegious. I thought it was brilliant. All of my financial modeling suggests it would double our profits again!

Phit: Your current executives have a very traditional perspective of what the industry is all about. They consider themselves as the guardians and stewards of the integrity of the profession. Early in your tenure your perspectives will have to be much more in alignment with their thinking.

Deputee: Oh.

Phit: Ms. Deputee, do you believe in Simply Secrets? Do you feel passionate about the company?

Deputee: Yes, absolutely. I am committed to the clandestine and covert cause. Without secrets, there would be no truth. Right, Doctor?

Phit: I see. So that's important to consider as well—you are a believer in the company, the mission, and the sales pitch. It makes you an effective prophet for the organization, both internally and externally.

Deputee: Hmmm, a secret female prophet . . . that sounds nice. I think I'll call Ms. Peoples now and tell her the good news.

Phit: One minute, Ms. Deputee. Remember the five things that you outlined at the beginning of our discussion, the five reasons why you most wanted to take this job?

Deputee: Yes. Are you going to make me eat my words?

Phit: It's just that I've been going through the file here. Have they made you a salary offer yet?

Deputee: Um . . .

Phit: I don't mean to be forward, but we're talking about your number five reason for taking the job, right? They must have offered you a ton of money.

Deputee: Actually, it's offered at my current salary. They said, you know, it's because I'm such an unknown commodity. They're taking a chance on me, and so on. I understand. There's the real potential for a big raise . . .

Phit: But nothing right away. I guess potential is not really as valued as you thought.

Deputee: True.

Phit: So, let's take number five off the table. Now, you said before that you were the power behind Mr. X's throne, is that right?

Deputee: Oh yeah.

Phit: So you had the power to make changes, get things done, and assume a leadership role. If that's the case, how does this new job offer any more power?

Deputee: I'll be the one calling the shots for the entire department. I'll be the one advocating my ideas directly. I can allocate resources, hire and fire, set policy within limit, without anyone else's approval.

Phit: So, let's leave number four on your list. Now, I cannot argue with your top reason: You want to be the first woman to achieve this goal. That is admirable, and obviously very important to you. So, we're left with three things.

Deputee: Culture change and prestige. And as we've talked, I've begun to wonder if there's much culture change possible. Maybe I can do something by example, by being a strong, empowered female executive. I don't know if that's going to help other women move up.

Phit: Perhaps one of the reasons you like Simply Secrets, the essential something that keeps you there, is the culture itself.

Maybe you like being the only woman in the boys' club. What if that club is a key component of its success. Are you still so sure that it has to be changed, and that you're the one to do it?

Deputee: That's deep stuff, Doc. I'd have to really think about that.

Phit: And what about prestige?

Deputee: I guess it only really matters outside the organization. If I wanted to use this job to jump into another one, or a different career, then the prestige factor would help. But I want to stay with Simply Secrets. I want my prestige to carry some weight there.

Phit: If we drop the rationale behind culture change and prestige is muddy, we're left with two, consistent reasons for taking the job.

Deputee: Yes.

Phit: And those reasons may be enough. In fact, they can be more than enough to overcome all these other Fit Gaps.

Deputee: This is going to be a tougher decision than I thought.

Phit: It always is, Ms. Deputee. I'll send you my report. It may help you make up your mind.

Chapter 14

Fit Assessment

Disclaimer: *As this book was going to press, the publisher received an unmarked package in the mail. Inside the package was a crude photocopy of Darlene Deputee's Fit Assessment form. The document also included notes and marginalia, presumably in the hand of Dr. Phineas Phit. The documents have all been authenticated. The publisher decided, in the interest of full disclosure, to include this fit assessment as an addendum to the book. Its contents may help readers better prepare for their next potential job opportunity.*

Classified Fit Report

Consultant:	Dr. Phineas Phit
Client:	Darlene Deputee
Company:	Simply Secrets
Date:	June 16, 2006

Scale: 1-5

FS=Fit Significance[1]

FI=Fit In Factor[2]

FG=Fit Gap[3]

---

[1] Indicates relative significance of a particular Fit Factor to the individual user

[2] Indicates individual's ability to "fit into" an environment or culture

[3] Measures the distance between FS and FI (formula: if FS≥FI, then FS=FI=FG; if FS≤FY, then FI-FS=FG)

Fit Factor:	Physical Package				
Fit Significance:	1	2	3	4	⑤
Fit In Factor	1	2	③	4	5
Fit Gap = 2					

Notes:

Ms. Deputee seems to understand the significance of the bias (euphemistically called "traditions") that she will confront. Her colleagues within the Simply Secrets culture are bound to be dismissive of her abilities. She seems to have the outside support necessary to sustain her. Does she actually want this challenge?

Fit Factor:	Powerful Patronage				
Fit Significance:	1	2	3	④	5
Fit In Factor	①	2	3	4	5
Fit Gap = 3					

Notes:

Darlene seems reluctant to secure the sponsorship of key executives. She needs to sell her ideas more effectively, but wants to make it on her own. None of the Simply Secrets executives has any experience in mentoring young women. It's highly unlikely that any board members will break ranks to lend her a hand.

Fit Factor:	Proper Pedigree				
Fit Significance:	①	2	3	4	5
Fit In Factor	1	2	3	④	5
Fit Gap = 3					

Notes:

Ms. Deputee is very proud of her academic record and her contemporary approach to the secrets industry. She tends to overemphasize her study with top researchers. She must be careful not to dwell on this at Simply Secrets; from what I hear, the executives are rooted in experience—not theory. Peoples overheard a few derisive comments about Deputee's "book learning."

Fit Factor:	Potential Performance				
Fit Significance:	1	2	③	4	5
Fit In Factor	1	2	3	④	5
Fit Gap = 1					

Notes:

Simply Secrets is in the process of changing its approach to hiring executives. This is the direct result of rapid growth. While they may understand intellectually that they will no longer be able to groom each new manager in the typical rotational process, they may not have embraced the idea systemically. My executive interviews suggest that they understand what it takes to properly staff the organization. They will probably see Deputee's advancement as evidence of this shift.

Fit Factor:	Proper Perspectives				
Fit Significance:	1	2	3	4	⑤
Fit In Factor	①	2	3	4	5
Fit Gap = 4					

Notes:

Ms. Deputee's education, experience, and freedom from convention allow her to innovate. She will make significant contributions to the bottom line. But her patience and savvy will be challenged because she does not understand the implications of directional shifts within the culture. Her colleagues on the Executive Board see her as being exclusively driven by profit. One executive told me—in confidence—that Deputee would "sell her mother to make a buck." There may be real misalignment here between this candidate and the culture.

Fit Factor:	Powerful Passion				
Fit Significance:	1	2	3	4	(5)
Fit In Factor	1	2	3	4	(5)
Fit Gap = 0					

Notes:

Simply Secrets and Deputee are in good alignment on this Fit Factor. She has sacrificed her personal life to follow her drive. She wants very much to be the first female executive in the industry. Deputee should downplay this drive, however; it may seem too aggressive for a woman in this culture.

Fit Factor:	Public Relations				
Fit Significance:	1	2	(3)	4	5
Fit In Factor	1	(2)	3	4	5
Fit Gap = 1					

Notes:

It's important to be highly regarded in the Simply Secrets culture. Deputee has to create buzz about her accomplishments—which may not come naturally. She seems willing to try.

Fit Factor:	Proper Passages				
Fit Significance:	1	2	3	4	(5)
Fit In Factor	1	(2)	3	4	5
Fit Gap = 3					

Notes:

As stated above, Simply Secrets is in a transition period—but change comes slowly for them. The current culture expects a slow rotation across all of the various departments, so senior executives can get to know the future leaders. The company has operated this way from the beginning. Deputee is the first "unknown" to be promoted from within. This is one of her biggest challenges.

Fit Factor:	Pastimes				
Fit Significance:	1	2	3	4	(5)
Fit In Factor	(1)	2	3	4	5
Fit Gap = 4					

Notes:

I feel sorry for Deputee. She's walking into an old boys' club, but she doesn't want to try to join in, or get along. She believes so strongly that performance merits respect, but it may not always work that way. There is an almost pathological unwillingness to compromise. She will not play golf, socialize, take vacations with co-workers, attend their clubs and churches, etc. It will inevitably compromise her insider knowledge of Simply Secrets.

Fit Factor:	Personal Presence				
Fit Significance:	1	2	3	④	5
Fit In Factor	①	2	3	4	5
Fit Gap = 3					

Notes:

This is another style mismatch. They fancy themselves a sales organization dedicated to wooing customers—Deputee is a technical expert focused on designing and delivering profitable products and services. If the organization ever shifted its expectations, this Fit Gap could be reduced, but it doesn't look positive.

Final Analysis:
TFG [Total Fit Gap] = 24 out of 40 ("Fit Challenge")

Scale:	
30-40	Fit Fight
20-29	Fit Challenge
10-19	Fit Neutral
0-9	Perfect Fit

Recommendation:

At first, this looked like a good match. But the more I discussed the matter—with Simply Secrets executives, with Ms. Peoples, and with Ms. Deputee herself, the more mismatches I saw. However, one cannot ignore the power of Deputee's drive and determination. That's not always enough to bridge a large Fit Gap, but it can be. I have to rely upon my data, my instincts, and thirty years of Fit Gap expertise in order to make my recommendation. I recommend. . . [4]

---

[4] This is where, tantalizingly, the document is cut off.

Survival or Fulfillment?

We may never learn the choice that Darlene Deputee made. Likewise, you will not be privy to the inside conversations, meetings, and decisions of leaders who decide your career fate. And you will not have a Certified Fit Consultant to help you gather secret intelligence on your prospective culture or your current job situation. Such tools exist only within the confines of this story.

But you will have something more—the understanding of "fit" as a decisive factor. You can also understand how informal rules and norms indicate what is happening within an organizational culture. If you use the Fit Factors to guide your choice, you can build a better career and create genuine fulfillment and well-being.

You can gather key information and intelligence from other sources (former and current employees, search consultants, media reports, legal filings) in order to supplement your research. Just remember the five key aspects of your Fit Scan:

1. **Core Values**: Knowing where you're starting from
2. **Identity Issues**: Understanding how certain identity issues (age, cultural background, education) affect how others experience you
3. **Motivators**: Knowing why you really want the job
4. **Organizational Fit Assessment**: Watching the Fit Factors play out in the prospective organization
5. **Fit Gap**: Accepting the degree to which you will have to adjust or compromise in order to fit in—and your willingness to do so.

Fulfillment vs. Survival

Without Fit, there are no intrinsically rewarding career paths available. Your sense of well-being will slowly erode. Your self-confidence, self esteem, sense of contribution, and vitality are all enhanced when your real self is in perfect alignment with your work environment. If you hide too much of your real self, you will suffer the emotional, spiritual, and psychological consequences over time. Besides, you deserve more than the routine day-to-day grind of an awkward, ill-fitting environment. You deserve to be in an environment where you can thrive and, above all, **Fit In!**

End Note

What did Dr. Phit recommend? Did Darlene take the job? And, most important of all, who leaked this story? Go back through the book, examine each character closely, and form your own theory. Then go to our website (www.identityonline.com) to vote for your answers. And **YOUR** choices will control what happens next.

Chapter 15

Afterword

In a world changing at an unrelenting pace, finding your place has become more difficult. As we continue to develop new so-called communication channels, it is too easy to underestimate the value of simple person-to-person interaction. If you can't understand, appreciate, and yes, even influence your fellow man, you may never achieve the success you dreamed of when you were young. The importance of understanding the rules, both spoken and unspoken, of the real world has become progressively more vital to our success both personally and professionally. The hard and cold truth is that each and every one of us must understand the lifelong importance of interacting with our fellow man.

From the time we are born through the end of our days, we each struggle in our own way to fit in and find our place in the world. Beginning with our first day of pre-school, through childhood and adolescence, and finally into adulthood, we each encounter situations where we must fit in. The new school, the new neighborhood, the new friends, the new job, the new co-workers, and the new boss—each presents a unique set of challenges that we must all face. Fitting in is so important that most of us remember our successes or failures with a vivid sense of either satisfaction or horror.

For most of us, the workplace, where we will spend the greatest percentage of our adult lives, will be the ultimate proving ground of our skill or lack thereof in fitting in. This simple corollary between our ability to fit in and our professional success is what makes Mark Williams' book so important.

Success in the workplace is too often seen as dependent on getting the right job, moving up the ladder, or meeting the right people in what appears to be a roulette wheel of fortune. Many of us look at workplace success and see a Vegas gambling table where a few lucky souls will win, but the majority will lose. Like gamblers in a casino, we continue to come and play, always hoping for the wheel to hit our number.

Mark Williams is a great thinker and storyteller and has done a masterful job of decoding the unwritten rules that govern the workplace. This book is useful to both employers and employees, as each can fall victim to the same pitfalls. In reading this book, I developed a more profound understanding of some of the choices I have made and how I can improve my company, my relationships with my staff and associates, and my personal life.

Having spent the majority of my adult life studying the opinions, attitudes, likes, dislikes, habits, and viewpoints of others, I can attest to the fact that most people have an overriding desire to succeed. So much of what we are and how we view ourselves as individuals can be seen on the yardstick we each measure ourselves against, indicating our successes and failures in the business world. Most people start, continue, and end that journey not knowing the pitfalls and tricks of the trail. This is what Mark has shown us all. His insightful classifications of the "Fit-In" traits give both the employer and the employee new tools to use that can make a real difference.

I wish you all the success you dream of.

—Michael Bach

Founder and CEO, Survey.com

Appendix 1

Fit Scan

The Background Check

Before you sign on the dotted line, conduct a culture scan to learn more about your prospective organization and your potential for a good fit. It's not difficult to get good information—it just takes a little time and effort. Your goal is to find out:

- What kind of people excel in that organization?
- What kind of people struggle there?
- Is it easy to figure out the informal rules?
- How quickly could you figure them out?
- How do you receive important feedback?
- Will you receive support?

Joining an organization is one of the most important decisions you can make. It will affect every aspect of your life, so take the time to learn as much as you can about your new home away from home before you make a commitment. Forget about awards, advertisements, and press releases designed to promote the brand of your prospective organization. Most companies are very adept at promoting their "image." You, however, want to decode their true "identity" to assess how you will fit into the day-to-day machinery of the organization.

Where Can You Gather Good Intelligence on Your Prospective Employer?

Below are some easy steps you can take to begin a thoughtful and comprehensive fit scan. After all, you can bet they'll do a pretty thorough background check on you; in today's world, you can't afford not to do the same.

Current and Former Employees

There's nothing like going straight to the horse's mouth to tease out the details of the informal rules operating in your prospective organization. Before you have an interview, find someone currently or previously on the inside to talk with about the informal norms. Keep in mind that their personal experience may not translate exactly to yours; and don't forget, their window on the world will color their experience of the organization.

Search Consultants/Head Hunters/Temp Agencies

Search consultants and temporary agencies can provide a goldmine of information about the culture of your prospective organization. They are charged with recruiting and identifying those outstanding candidates who most closely fit the corporate cultures of their clients. Their professional observations can prove invaluable for you as they hear many anecdotal stories that reveal patterns of the types of people who succeed in various organizations.

Vendors/Partners

Suppliers and alliance partners have bird's eye views of organizations because they navigate the maze of formal and informal rules in order to conduct business with your prospective employer. They could provide helpful insights into the personality of the culture, as well as offer points of comparison with their other business clients.

Personal Visit to Headquarters/Facilities

You can learn a lot by just walking around the lobby of the company you're interested in joining. Observe the clues provided there, such as employee dress and mannerisms, staff interaction and tone, and the nature and style of the décor. Although subtle, these indicators speak loudly about the personality of the company.

Employment Interviews

When called for an interview by either a company representative or a hired recruiter, listen closely to the formal and informal questions you are asked. Take note of which P's are present in the queries of your interviewer. They indicate what matters to the company's culture. Once a client proudly shared with me that when she was being interviewed for a mid-level management job with a Fortune 50 company, the interviewer asked about her participation in college athletics. She shared that she had played college basketball for a Division 2 championship team and the interviewer said, "That's the kind of spirit we look for."

Fit Scan Questions

■ **Packaging** (your look, appearance, physical and cultural attributes)

Is there a preferred look for the people who have been successful in the organization?

■ **Pedigree** (your background, heritage, credentials)

Are there any patterns that emerge when you assess the backgrounds of those who have been successful?

■ **Patronage** (your advocates, allies, friends in high places)

Is it necessary/ easy to find a mentor or someone to guide you in the organization?

■ Perspective (your point of view, values, beliefs)

Are employees expected to toe the party line? Are alternative opinions, voices, and perspectives encouraged?

■ **Pastimes** (your leisure activities, social activities)

Are there any particular leisure activities or sports that are preferred by employees? Is it important to participate in those pastimes in order to be seen as a team player?

■ **Passion** (your drive, ambition, will to succeed)

How much of your life do you have to commit to the organization in order to be seen as a vital contributor? Is there flexibility based on the stage of life you are in?

■ **Presence** (your style, demeanor, attitude, charisma)

Is there a noticeable style that people who are successful seem to have?

■ **Potential** (your perceived raw talent, intelligence)

How important is it to be seen as a rising star or hot talent in order to succeed?

■ **PR** (your image, reputation, aura)

How much time and effort do you have to spend promoting yourself, attaining visibility, and being seen by the "right people"?

■ **Passages** (your pathways, tickets to be punched, ways up the corporate ladder)

Are the career paths well defined or flexible? How hard is it to get your tickets punched?

Give yourself the gift of a "fit scan." Take the time to investigate the informal rules of the culture you're about to join. If you find your fit, your gifts will be recognized, your teammates will benefit from your energy and spirit, and you'll reap rich rewards because the environment will nurture your abilities.

Appendix 2

Strategies for Dealing with Fit Fights

So, what can you do once you know you're "swimming upstream?" You have choices and probably a lot of support, as well. Here's how the 799 people who responded to the Fit In Survey (conducted by Survey.com) rated various options. If you're currently engaged in a Fit Fight, your solution may be listed below. Remember, Fit Fights are exhausting, so make sure you activate your support system and seek advice from people who have been in your situation before.

"Stay, but actively look for another job that's a better fit."

Survey.com Fit In Survey: (48%; n=386)

Obviously, this is the strategy of choice for most people. The benefits are numerous. Once you've made the decision to leave, you will find that your level of internal stress immediately declines, even though you remain in your current workplace. When you find a new opportunity, you give proper notice, being sure not to burn bridges and avoiding financial hits.

Tip: *Careful with your openness about your plans—most high fit cultures will freeze you out if they find you're looking for another job, unless they really want you to leave.*

"Stay and try to refocus other's attention towards your abilities."

Survey.com Fit In Survey: (26%; n=208)

To fully utilize this solution, it's a good idea to first be clear about your successful outcomes, work product, accomplishments, and contributions. It's also a good idea to remind your employer about happy internal clients you've groomed. The challenge here is to refrain from launching a consuming crusade about yourself, possibly making yourself sick from trying to convince the organization you're doing a good job. In an organization that's heavily vested in upholding the informal aspects of its culture, you're wasting your time. Rather, try all your change options internally first—sometimes the right supervisor can make all the difference towards guaranteeing your success. A transfer to another manager with fresh eyes could also make a difference.

Tip: *Make a clearheaded, hardnosed assessment of how tied the organization is to maintaining status quo.*

"Stay Because You Need the Job."

Survey.com Fit In Survey: (11%; n=88)

If financial responsibility is a primary factor, you just may need to stay put for a while. On the contrary, if you're on a particular career track, it is probably not wise to mark time for too long in an environment where you're swimming upstream. Your self-esteem and confidence could suffer as the internal stress pulls you down. If, however, the most important dimensions of your life are outside work and you don't seek to derive major life satisfaction from your job (other than your salary), you could choose to stay and learn to tolerate the situation until something better comes along as you outwait the situation.

Tip: *Make sure your life outside of work offers needed support and rejuvenation. It's always helpful, on many levels, to talk to lots of people—sometimes your own network can help you find a new job.*

"Resign immediately. The organization isn't worth it!"

Survey.com Fit In Survey: (5%; n=40)

The good news about pursuing this solution is that you will extricate yourself from the negative situation. Assuming you've thought through the financial implications of this strategy, by resigning you'd be free to focus on the next key steps towards identifying a better fit. The down side is that if you're not cautious and if you need to use your former employer as a reference, the fit issues you've struggled with could emerge in a reference discussion with a potential new employer. This would not set the positive tone you want in starting a new position.

Tip: *Leave without burning bridges.*

"Start your own company and create the 'perfect fit' for you."

Survey.com Fit In Survey (2%; n=19)

More and more people are doing this every year. But be warned—you have to be prepared! If you think this is a viable choice for you, use the time at your current job to incubate your ideas. It takes dedication, perseverance, capital, and a high tolerance for risk to be self-employed. Make sure the entrepreneurial lifestyle is one that "fits" with your personality.

"Retire."

Survey.com Fit In Survey: (2%; n=14)

This is a big life decision. To leave your workplace is a significant disruption, but to leave work all together is a life altering move—one that you need to have thought through completely with lots of expert advice, family input, and advance planning.

Tip: *As Boomers leave the workplace, they will "rewire," not retire. Finding a new work interest, learning new skills, and applying your talents to different endeavors may be other options that appeal to you.*

Additional Ideas to Solve Fit Fights

Job Counseling: Many organizations have career development counselors on hand who can help you determine if you need a change of scene or a change of organization. Before you make a big decision, use all of the available resources your current employer offers to fully explore your options.

Temporary Work: Many temporary organizations offer an opportunity to explore corporate environments without having to make a long-term commitment. In this scenario, you can do your own research on the many kinds of corporations, styles of work, and informal cultures out there while still being paid. Temporary work helps you avoid the downside of being enmeshed in just one culture while simultaneously meeting your financial obligations.

Sabbatical: There are lots of ways to take a sabbatical if your company allows it. You can explore available options, such as company-sponsored educational programs that send you back to school or that offer a temporary work alternative in a community service program. These are particularly effective strategies if you're feeling stuck with a bad manager or supervisor, but hope to remain with your current organization.

Appendix 3

Human Resources Fit Audit

Half of Respondents Won't Tolerate Bad Fit

The best approach HR leaders can take to eliminat unnecessary fit requirements (like being tall for a presidential candidate) is to ensure that an organization's systems and policies are *implemented as they are designed and intended.* It is rare for the formal systems in today's organizations to deliberately limit or exclude. Rather, unnecessary fit requirements may lurk unknowingly in the minds of the managers and supervisors charged with implementing those policies and systems. Most managers and supervisors do not intentionally subvert an organization's stated desires, but they must respond flexibly to the reality of the business demands and outcomes they are accountable for. A gap may exist between the high ideals of leaders as mandated in their progressive policies and the daily realities of conducting business.

To address limiting fit requirements, the gap must be acknowledged and dealt with aggressively. Why would any HR leader want to undertake such difficult and challenging work?

According to a yearlong study conducted by McKinsey & Company involving seventy-seven companies and almost 6,000 managers and executives, the most important corporate resource over the next twenty years will be talent: smart, sophisticated business people who are technologically literate, globally astute, and operationally agile. And as the demand for talent goes up, the supply will go down.

According to *Fast Company*, the McKinsey team is very frank about the results of these trends. In its report entitled "The War for Talent," the search for the best and the brightest will become a constant, costly battle—a fight with no final victory.

Not only will companies have to devise more imaginative hiring practices; they will also have to work harder to keep their best people. In the new economy, competition is global, capital is abundant, ideas are developed quickly and cheaply, and people are willing to change jobs often. In that kind of environment, says Ed Michaels, a McKinsey director who helped manage the study, "All that matters is talent. Talent wins."

OUR FIT STUDY FOUND THE FOLLOWING RESULTS:

Total Answering	799	100%
Stay/actively look for another job that's a better fit	386	48%
Stay/try to refocus others' attention towards your abilities	208	26%
Stay because you need the job	88	11%
Resign immediately—the organization isn't worth it	40	5%
Don't know	32	4%
Start your own company and create the "perfect fit" for you	19	2%
Other	12	2%
Retire	14	1%

These results indicate that 5 percent of employees will leave immediately and 48 percent of employees won't tolerate a bad fit, but will stay in a job until they secure alternative employment. Think of the lost productivity resulting from employees silently and secretly looking for new opportunities while still having significant responsibility for your bottom line. It certainly makes good business sense to eliminate unnecessary fit requirements that may create barriers so that your talent stays contented and productive. Additional reasons why HR executives should consider fit audits:

1. Many Fit Factors are unnecessary to the functioning of the business. With an impending war on talent, you need every edge to keep employees with experience and talent in your organization.

2. Many Fit Factors are rooted in individual bias. When informal fit requirements are inconsistently applied to members of protected identity groups, your organization may become vulnerable to claims of bias.

3. Talented people are sometimes silently excluded and screened out. If it's innovation you want, then firm fit requirements are what you need. Harness your employees to strictly follow company rules so as to filter out their personal preferences.

Fit In!

4. Employees who are in Fit Fights are not as productive as you need. They're spending a great deal of psychic and intellectual time trying to learn, adapt to, and navigate a system of informal norms that have nothing to do with the core business. Many Fit Factors support the nostalgic style and life circumstances of the workforce of days gone by.

No matter how good the formal policy, if managers who implement the polices cannot see a connection between them and the bottom line, they will at least give them lip service or at best, half-hearted, uneven implementation. It takes a real commitment to work through cultural issues in addition to courage, direction, and support from the top—not to mention, significant resources. If you choose to audit the impact of your organization's informal norms, check out these examples of the "reality versus ideal" gap. Below are some examples of this gap that is frequently only whispered about. See if you can identify where you or your organization places on the continuum. The closer you position your organization toward the "reality" end, the greater the gap between the credibility and real effectiveness of your policies.

Fit Audit

Recruitment Ideal: *"We are looking for diversity of thought to spur innovation."*

Recruitment Reality: People who are too far "out the box" or who are not perceived as being equipped to "hit the ground running" will be bypassed by hiring managers.

Impact: Your recruiters will return with candidates who fulfill the "real" mandate. They will not risk the punishment of fulfilling the "ideal" objective—unless they are truly rewarded for it! Consider whether the hiring managers are really required to take a serious look at "alterative candidates." As you know, managers will not hire "experiments."

> **Is your organization closer to the ideal or the reality?**
>
> Fit Ideal————————————————————Fit Reality

Mentoring Ideal: *"We want all kinds of people to succeed, so we will formalize our mentoring program to offer those who may not have access to a mentor the chance to benefit from an experienced perspective."*

Mentoring Reality: Executives dutifully participate in the formal mentoring program, but continue to identify and nourish their own selected emerging talent under the radar.

Impact: There is a two track system for patronage—one is formal, the other is invisible.

> **Is your organization closer to the ideal or the reality?**
>
> Fit Ideal————————————————————Fit Reality

Performance Feedback Ideal: *"We like to give our employees direct feedback through a formal performance appraisal process."*

Performance Feedback Reality: Managers use clichés like, "You need to work on your team skills" or "improve you communications skills" to avoid difficult fit discussions they are not prepared to handle, especially those conversations across identity differences.

Impact: Many employees never get straight feedback about their fit challenges because of the potential legal implications or because of the discomfort of the managers.

> **Is your organization closer to the ideal or the reality?**
>
> Fit Ideal————————————————Fit Reality

Career Advancement Ideal: *"We have a formal posting process that gives everyone an opportunity to apply for a job, assuming they meet all the requirements."*

Career Advancement Reality: Behind the scenes, people have been prepared and positioned to assume certain jobs. There is lots of talk about who the "real candidates" are by those responsible for making the final decision.

Impact: Employees get the feeling that jobs are "wired;" their chance of advancement depends more on who they know than what they know or may have accomplished.

> **Is your organization closer to the ideal or the reality?**
>
> Fit Ideal————————————————Fit Reality

Work-Life Programs and Policies Ideal: *"We promote work-life balance for our employees with programs such as telecommuting, job sharing, parental leave, etc."*

Work-Life Programs and Policies Reality: With shrinking resources, layoffs, and pressures to do more with less, only the work warriors have access to real opportunity.

Impact: Those who utilize family friendly policies are viewed as less productive, not as reliable and less central.

> **Is your organization closer to the ideal or the reality?**
>
> Fit Ideal————————————————————Fit Reality

Fast Track Diversity Programs Ideal: *"We want to foster a diverse work environment to leverage the differences."*

Fast Track Diversity Programs Reality: Diversity candidates with access to fast track opportunities are viewed as not having paid their dues and are accepted through the traditional career path as "tokens."

Impact: Diversity candidates are challenged to get the support and legitimacy they need to succeed in the company.

> **Is your organization closer to the ideal or the reality?**
>
> Fit Ideal————————————————————Fit Reality

Ensure to Insure

The best insurance that your organization offers a fair shot at advancement includes the following:

- Be sure that the critical systems and polices affecting the culture and informal rules are consistently and fairly implemented;
- Be sure there are no "winks and nods" that undercut their effectiveness; and
- Be sure that actual competencies, skills, and observable results are rewarded.

Fit
Research

Markus Works commissioned Survey.com to conduct a study in order to assess respondents' perceptions of how significant a series of informal and unwritten rules are in creating barriers to their success in their organizations. The survey also sought to identify how respondents would react if their inability to "fit in" made it difficult for them to advance in the workplace.

Research Methodology

An online survey was conducted to collect the data for this study. The survey was fielded from August 2 to August 8, 2006. An e-mail invitation with an embedded link to the survey yielded a total of 800 completed surveys.

Research Findings

Demographic Profile

- Respondents tended to be Caucasian (59%), female (64%), and less than 50 years old (76%).

- The vast majority of respondents attended at least some college (**91%**).

		% of Total Population
Gender	Male	35%
	Female	64%
Age	18 – 34	36%
	35 – 49	40%
	50 – 64	24%
	65 or older	1%
Ethnicity	Caucasian	59%
	African American	14%
	Asian/Pacific Islander	14%
	Hispanic/Latino	9%
	Native American/Alaskan Native	2%
	Multi-racial	2%
Education Level	Graduate school (degree)	23%
	Some graduate school	7%
	College (degree)	35%
	Some college	26%
	High school (diploma/GED)	9%
	Middle school/junior high school	0%

Table 1. Q1, Q2, Q12-Q16—Demographic profile.
(Total population, n=794-800)

- In addition to these demographic breakouts, results indicated that 21% of respondents held management or executive roles.

The Ten Fit Factors

Respondents were asked to rate a series of items (the Ten Fit Factors) on the extent to which they create barriers to their success in their current organizations.

- The total population rated Passion (**27%**), PR (**26%**), and Perspectives (**25%**) as the top barriers to their success. Packaging (**15%**), Pedigree (15%), and Pastimes (**10%**) were not considered significant barriers (Figure 1).

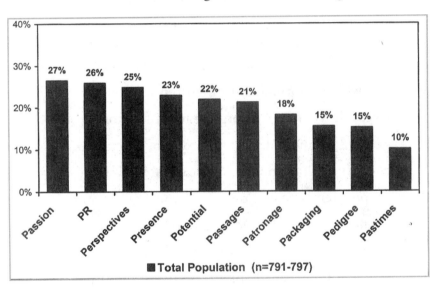

Figure 1. Q1-Q10. **Please rate each of the following on the extent to which informal and unwritten rules create barriers to your success in your current organization. (Bottom 2 box scores)**

- With the exceptions of Passion, Packaging, and Pastimes, females scored the Fit Factors higher than males for creation of barriers in their current organizations (Figure 2).

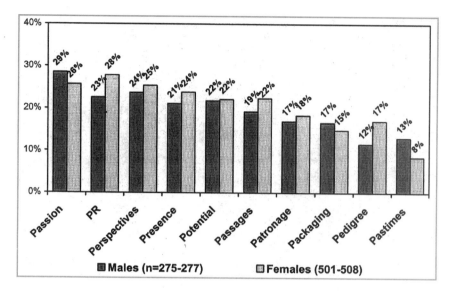

Figure 2. Q1-Q10. Please rate each of the following on the extent to which informal and unwritten rules create barriers to your success in your current organization. (Bottom 2 box scores)

- Results indicated a downward trend in barriers as respondents age; the youngest respondents (18- to 34-year-olds) consistently scored the Fit Factors highest among all age groups, while the oldest group (50-year-olds and older) tended to score the Fit Factors the lowest.

- There was a small spike among data for "Potential," in which both the youngest and oldest groups report barriers created (Figure 3).

Fit In!

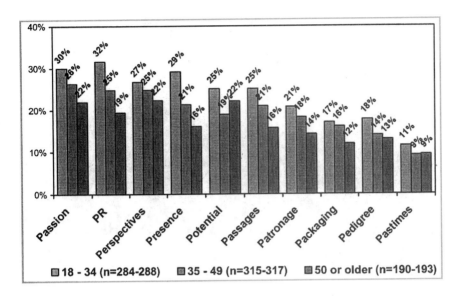

Figure 3. Q1-Q10. Please rate each of the following on the extent to which informal and unwritten rules create barriers to your success in your current organization. (Bottom 2 box scores)

- Results show Asian and Pacific Islanders generally rated the Fit Factors the highest for creation of barriers, especially for PR (43%), Passion (37%), and Presence (36%).
- African Americans rated Packaging (24%) and Pedigree (21%) the highest among all ethnic groups for creation of barriers to the success in their current organization (Figure 4).

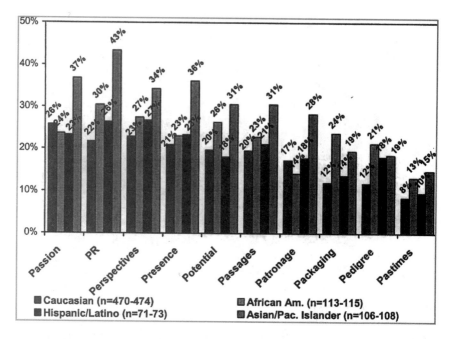

Figure 4. Q1-Q10. Please rate each of the following on the extent to which informal and unwritten rules create barriers to your success in your current organization. (Bottom 2 box scores)

■ In general, results by industry were similar to those of the total population.

■ Respondents from most industries and job titles identified Passion as one of the top barriers to their success within their organizations (22%–33%). However, respondents employed by the government did not identify Passion as one of their most significant barriers.

■ Packaging, Pedigree, and Pastimes were not indicated by respondents (regardless of industry or job title) to be significant barriers. (Table 2)

Fit In!

	Passion	PR	Perspectives	Presence	Potential	Passages	Patronage	Packaging	Pedigree	Pastimes
Total answering	27%	26%	25%	23%	22%	21%	18%	15%	15%	10%
INDUSTRY:										
Manufacturing/consumer products	25%	22%	30%	25%	27%	25%	20%	17%	16%	11%
Communications	26%	22%	19%	15%	33%	22%	7%	19%	15%	0%
Education	22%	21%	27%	22%	19%	19%	22%	14%	18%	12%
Financial services/insurance/real estate	26%	22%	22%	20%	23%	21%	26%	12%	12%	5%
Healthcare/pharmaceuticals	31%	33%	26%	21%	23%	25%	15%	18%	16%	8%
IT	33%	34%	34%	34%	27%	32%	22%	17%	22%	23%
Government	18%	28%	28%	17%	21%	18%	14%	15%	12%	10%
Retail/wholesale	28%	35%	26%	26%	18%	25%	20%	11%	15%	11%
Services	29%	23%	21%	32%	13%	18%	15%	18%	13%	9%
Transportation/utilities	26%	13%	21%	24%	21%	21%	18%	11%	16%	11%
Other	30%	28%	21%	22%	23%	18%	15%	18%	15%	11%
JOB TITLE:										
C-level/owner/president	23%	26%	16%	23%	18%	18%	14%	18%	20%	18%
Marketing/sales	23%	23%	20%	24%	18%	18%	21%	18%	15%	13%
Finance/accounting	26%	27%	24%	26%	19%	24%	23%	13%	16%	5%
Other management	23%	25%	23%	16%	21%	21%	15%	12%	16%	10%
Administration	32%	26%	28%	21%	24%	23%	19%	17%	24%	8%
IT	33%	27%	34%	29%	28%	29%	22%	18%	14%	14%
Other	25%	26%	24%	22%	22%	19%	17%	15%	12%	9%

Table 2. Q1-Q10. Please rate each of the following on the extent to which informal and unwritten rules create barriers to your success in your current organization. (Bottom 2 box scores)

"What would you do?"

Respondents were then asked what they would do if their inability to fit in made it difficult to advance (Table 3).

- The majority (**85%**) of respondents would stay at their job in some form.
- Nearly half (**48%**) of all respondents would stay and actively look for another job if their inability to fit in made it difficult to advance.

	% of Total Population
Stay/actively look for another job that's a better fit	48%
Stay/try to refocus others' attention towards your abilities	26%
Stay because you need the job	11%
Resign immediately – the organization isn't worth it	5%
Don't know	4%
Start your own company and create the "perfect fit" for you	2%
Retire	2%
Other	2%

Table 3. Q11. Now that you have answered a number of questions about fitting in with your organization, what would you do if your inability to fit in made it difficult to advance?

About the Author

Mark Williams is a bestselling author, dynamic speaker, and experienced consultant and educator. His expertise spans vital issues such as identity, cross-cultural understanding, organizational development, global tolerance, and personal growth. Mark's hallmark is the communication of innovative ideas through a creative blending of multimedia and interactive technology as well as original research. Mark is the Founder of *Identity Online*, a broadband network created to distribute educational programming, research, e-learning, and information related to complex identity and diversity challenges.

Mr. Williams has provided consultation for a wide variety of clients, including Exxon Corporation, AT & T, the U.S. Department of Defense, Federal Aviation Administration, Colgate Palmolive, the Agency for International Development, the Central Intelligence Agency, Microsoft, Harvard Medical School, UNISYS, Cisco Systems, Office Depot, Microsoft, EDS and dozens of other Fortune 500 companies. He has been quoted widely in business publications such as *Fast Company*, *Black Enterprise*, and in *The Boston Globe*, *San Francisco Chronicle*, and *Chicago Tribune*. He has appeared as a guest on national television programs including *Bloomberg News*, CBS's *The Early Show*, and the CNN Financial News Network.

Mark Williams is the author of *The 10 Lenses: Your Guide to Living and Working in a Multicultural World* (Capital Books, 2001) and *Your Identity Zones* (Capital, 2004).